P9-CKS-649

To LARRY
FROM
DAVE + VIC
XMAS 07

An Extraordinary

Friendship at the End of Life

Arthur Motyer

with Elma Gerwin

& Carol Shields

THE

STAIRCASE

LETTERS

RANDOM HOUSE CANADA

Copyright © 2007 Arthur Motyer

All rights reserved under International and Pan-American Copyright Conventions. No part of this book may be reproduced in any form or by any electronic or mechanical means, including information storage and retrieval systems, without permission in writing from the publisher, except by a reviewer, who may quote brief passages in a review. Published in 2007 by Random House Canada, a division of Random House of Canada Limited. Distributed in Canada by Random House of Canada Limited.

Random House Canada and colophon are trademarks.

www.randomhouse.ca

Library and Archives Canada Cataloguing in Publication

Motyer, Arthur
The staircase letters : an extraordinary friendship at the end of life /
Arthur Motyer ; with Elma Gerwin & Carol Shields.

ISBN 978-0-307-35640-6

1. Motyer, Arthur—Correspondence. 2. Gerwin, Elma—Correspondence.
3. Shields, Carol, 1935-2003—Correspondence. I. Gerwin, Elma
II. Shields, Carol, 1935–2003 III. Title.

PS8626.O8468Z546 2007   C813'.6   C2007-903029-7

Eliot, T.S. "The Journey of the Magi", *Collected Poems 1909–1962*. London: Faber and Faber, 2002. Used by permission.

Shapiro, Karl. "A Cut Flower", *The Wild Card: Selected Poems, Early and Late*. University of Illinois Press, 1998. Used by permission of the author.

Excerpted from *Unless* by Carol Shields. Copyright © 2002 Carol Shields Literary Trust. Reprinted by permission of Random House Canada.

Extracted from *The Stone Diaries* by Carol Shields. Copyright © 1993 Carol Shields Literary Trust. Reprinted by permission of Random House Canada.

Extracted from *The Republic of Love* by Carol Shields. Copyright © 1992 Carol Shields Literary Trust. Reprinted by permission of Random House Canada.

Carol Shields's correspondence is reproduced with the kind permission of the Carol Shields Literary Trust.

The e-mail correspondence that appears in this work was in no way written with the intent of publication.

Printed and bound in the United States of America

10 9 8 7 6 5 4 3 2 1

In memory of
Elma and Carol

And for Alasdair, Michael and Gillian

IT WAS AFTER the death of Carol Shields, following that of Elma Gerwin, that I re-read their many e-mails to me over the previous two years, and realized again how truly special that correspondence was. After gathering the letters together, I was grateful to secure publication approval from Donald Shields and Martin Gerwin.

During the last years of her life, Carol made it clear that she did not want to be used for publicity about cancer that might draw attention to herself. In her dying, however, she has left in these letters, as

Elma has, an inspiring example of how the ending of life can be faced. These were two extraordinary women, one an established literary icon, the other highly literate but known only to her friends, and their story deserves a wide sharing.

ARTHUR MOTYER
Sackville, New Brunswick
2007

ONE

Happiness is the lucky pane of glass you carry
in your head. It takes all your cunning just to
hang on to it, and once it's smashed you have
to move into a different sort of life.

—From *Unless*

SPIRALLING TOWARDS DEATH, she stretched out her hand. Icarus falling, crying out but not to family. Husband, children, in-laws, all of them loving, would be there to cushion the fall when it came. She knew that. Pick up the pieces, bury them, burn them, give them to science. They would know what to do. Her cry was to others, two in particular, one man, one woman, as she began her free-fall flight. Her name was Elma Gerwin. I was the man. Carol Shields was the woman.

Forty years earlier, Elma had been a student of mine in English at Bishop's University in Lennoxville,

3

Quebec, and brilliant she was, too, challenging me constantly to look deeper, go further, and share with her immediately anything new I learned. A short, slight figure with a look sharp enough to pierce a steel door, she would fix me with her eyes, whether I was pacing about in a lecture room or sitting at a seminar table, and make escape impossible. Not that I wanted to escape. I was, after all, supposed to be the one in charge. I was fifteen years older, I was tall, I was (some said) commanding, and I had a big voice. Yet Elma was the one who held me in thrall. Her own voice was never soft, gentle, and low, as Cordelia's appeared to Lear, but neither was it shrill: it suited her as an excellent weapon of communication, reinforced and toned down with a smile.

I never cast Elma in any of the plays I produced as the university's director of drama, because she had no aspirations as an actress and preferred to do make-up. *She Stoops to Conquer*, *The Diary of Anne Frank*, Giraudoux's *The Enchanted*, Obey's Noah, were all plays I did at the time; and I can see her now, dressed in a borrowed white lab coat, too long and too big for her small figure, bending over an actor seated in front of a mirror, transforming a young face into an old one with a few liners and sticks of greasepaint held in her hands. It was in the classroom, however, that she showed how much she cared for the power of words. Writers were her gods. Victorian thinkers—Newman, Carlyle, Ruskin, among others—were her passion, as were the poets, all of them her friends: Shakespeare, Milton, Wordsworth, Tennyson, Hopkins, Yeats. She read them all.

Inevitably, in the years that followed her graduation, we lost touch, lengthy letters to each other giving way to the annual note tucked inside a Christmas card, sometimes with a photograph. She had married a philosopher, and they lived in Winnipeg. I knew that. They had three children. I knew that. She still read everything. I might have guessed that. But only gradually over the years did I learn that she had become a tireless advocate for literacy, and she worked with students in special programs. She had become a supporter of the New Democratic Party. She had a genuine concern for Aboriginal peoples. She went into and came out of a ten-year period as an alcoholic. She raged at injustices, wherever perceived. But she still loved a world that provoked her to fight in it, ignorance and prejudice always her enemies.

In late February 2001, I wrote to Elma about a literary matter. I had written two novels, one of which, *Swing Wide the Door*, was about a gay Salvation Army officer, trapped in an organization he felt was homophobic. I hoped she would agree to read the manuscript, because her acute critical judgment was something I knew I could trust. She had known for years that I was gay, so I had no anxieties that she would be shocked by the subject. Her immediate and helpful response by e-mail—established by now as a faster and more reliable form of communication between us in urgent times—confirmed her place as valued critic and friend. She quickly, and correctly, pointed out that one particular incident involving a prostitute was one she'd read in other forms and that to avoid cliché I would have to give it a new twist: "The fact that something has often happened in real life does not mean it will work well in fiction. Trite but true—yes, I know." She went on to suggest some valuable rethinking for the novel.

I was not, however, prepared for what she had to say so frankly about herself. Earlier that year, a multitude of polyps had been discovered in her colon, some of them of the kind that lead frequently to cancer. Because major surgery to remove a section of her colon had not been immediately proposed, she faced the prospect of repeated colonoscopies (invasive diagnostic procedures) and polypectomies (the surgery that snips off the precancerous polyps). Although not yet aware that a small-cell cancer was also growing in her lung—it would be diagnosed six months later, in September, and was one that could readily metastasize—she was able to have an early sense of what was ahead of her, and she was obviously determined to make this her last fight.

She told me she had written to Carol Shields, whom she had known and admired when they'd both lived in Winnipeg. Carol, who now lived in Victoria, had been diagnosed with breast cancer in 1998. And now Elma wrote to me. We were, she assured us, two very important people in her life—people she could count on to accept and understand what was happening to her—and her proposal was that we make a special journey together.

The medieval Everyman had made a similar request:

I shall show you how it is:
Commanded I am to go a journey,
A long way, hard and dangerous,
And give a straight count without delay
Before the high judge Adonai.
Wherefore I pray you bear me company.

Elma lived in the middle of Canada, I was on the east coast, Carol on the west, but e-mail could link us easily. Elma would write to both of us at once, or any one of us would write to the other, and we three would travel together, bear each other company, and give a straight account without delay.

With wax melting in the sun, it would be a perilous voyage.

I am now the lone survivor.

Elma had made sure that Carol Shields knew something about me, but I had not met her, except in her books. This meant, however, that I knew a few things about her. She, too, had been a teacher, a professor at the University of Ottawa, the University of

British Columbia, and the University of Manitoba, as well as being one of Canada's truly great writers, someone who reminded us again "why literature matters," which is what *The New York Times Book Review* said of her Pulitzer Prize–winning *Stone Diaries* in 1993. For that novel and others that followed, Carol was either nominated for or awarded some of the world's great literary prizes, her repertoire extending to poems, short stories, plays, and literary criticism.

Carol was someone Elma deeply loved, but she also made it clear that she loved something in me, though what exactly and why? We might tell someone why we love them, but to tell ourselves why we are loved may prove only a searching excuse for vanity. In one of his early poems, beginning "When you are old and grey and full of sleep," Yeats speaks of "the pilgrim soul" found in a beloved. Unspecific though that is, it may yet be the only way to articulate the impossible.

In this my eighty-second year, I look back on my own years as a teacher, aware that I won't be a survivor for another four decades of teaching. Even if I were, there would not be time enough to understand whatever it was I did for Elma or for anyone else, or even how or why I did it. It amazes me to hear of teachers who profess answers for what can never be known and what is forever beyond reach. For my part, I had no method unless it was to care. I had no philosophy or formal structure of ideas, unless it was to make a teacher different from a book. Is this why Elma turned to me, despite her love of books, knowing that I wasn't a book? Was this the "pilgrim soul" she may have found in me?

It was Michael Ondaatje who wrote: "All my life I've admired teachers, those mysterious catalysts, fathers without a bloodline, those who point out an unknown field or surprising city over the horizon. Leonard Cohen, for instance, spoke of Irving Layton this way: 'I taught him how to dress. He taught me how to live.'"

If I ever pointed out to Elma or any other student such a field or such a surprising city, it may have been that I didn't know it was there myself until I saw it.

When Elma was a student, I had introduced her to Mahler with a recording I had of Kathleen Ferrier singing *Das Lied von der Erde (The Song of the Earth)*. She had been moved deeply by the last song, "Der Abschied," where the poet bids his long farewell to life.

> *Still is my heart. It is awaiting its hour!*
> *Everywhere the lovely earth blossoms*
> *forth in spring and grows green anew!*
> *Everywhere, for ever, horizons are blue and bright!*
> *For ever and ever.*

Listening, we were both struck by the sheer beauty of all that loveliness fading away almost to nothing, but never really fading away at all, not ever . . . ewig . . . ewig . . . ewig. And that is the way we would end all our letters to each other thereafter . . . ewig . . . ewig . . . ewig . . . and all our e-mails to each other in the last months of her life . . . ever . . . ever . . . ever . . . our pledge that the world would remain green.

Despite sensing my own lack of qualifications for the role Elma was asking me to play—after all, she and Carol shared the prognosis of cancer while my health was fine—I said yes, I would try. And so it was that, after reflecting further on *Swing Wide the*

Door, the novel she had so helpfully criticized, she sent a long e-mail:

> Oh Arthur, you poor man, you started something up again when you wrote me that touchingly tentative letter asking me if I would consider reading your book. I had forgotten how much I missed being in regular contact with you—not the Christmas card stuff, but the feeling of being able to tell you almost anything with the assurance that you would understand—or at least tolerate.
>
> Is there anyone else I could have talked to so freely about the fact that nature probably intended me to be bisexual, for example? (Now there's another road not taken.) And just as much, if not more, I have missed seeing your handwriting on an envelope, knowing that whatever you had to say would be worth pondering, that always the essence would be there, and that it would be instinct with love.
>
> Do you think I don't know how it feels to be approaching the end of one's life with the feeling, "Surely I could have, even should

have, accomplished more than this? Left some monument, however small, more lasting than bronze?" (That colossal wreck of Shelley's Ozymandias in the sands is hardly comfort. Something more lasting than a human memory might be more like it anyway.) And I may be fourteen years younger than you, but I have my doubts I'll live as long—nor as well. I can try to put a good face on it, but I have to say I'm a bit scared after this latest finding.

Mind you, there is a silver lining. I could have developed Parkinson's like my mother; or the emphysema, which is my legacy of forty plus years of smoking, might have killed me through rapid lung-function degeneration (though I enjoyed smoking immensely, goddamn it, especially when I had to quit drinking. At least I can still have an occasional cigarette without spiralling out of control, which is emphatically not true in the case of alcohol).

Maybe the earth goddess is giving me an out. I won't have to start saving up sleeping pills or whatever: I can refuse to go on having colonoscopies and polypectomies and let nature take its course—and just hope that in my case colon cancer develops and metastasizes fairly quickly. Does this sound self-pitying? Probably. But I would be sincerely grateful to have an alternative to Parkinson's, especially. My poor mom, with her basically strong constitution, living for so long in that ghastly cage. I simply don't think I have that much courage—or that much faith.

I do feel sorry for you reading all this whining! At least it's been a help to me just to write it out. I'll leave it for tonight and read it again later. I guess I had a rather off-putting day, which began bright and early with having yet more blood tests for various things (and I'm always so cheery at 8 a.m. anyway, of course), and then went on to become one of those days at work that leave you feeling exhausted, frustrated and as if there's no point whatsoever to anything you're doing (or have ever done).

Strange, isn't it, that while it means much to hear (and even occasionally believe!) that one has been a good parent, partner, teacher, whatever, there is still the desire to have created some small thing of value which is more . . . concrete? tangible? How we do ache to see our words made flesh—and with at least a measure of grace and truth.

"And not breed one work that wakes . . ." was Hopkins's own anguished summary of failure. Oh yes, I know, believe me, I know. Indeed, I look at your accomplishments and I only wish I could leave a legacy such as yours. It's all relative, no? "Send *my* roots rain," indeed.

Ever . . . ever . . . ever . . .

E.

P.S., or maybe a preface:

I might mention that the mood of this letter has probably been affected by my hearing of the death (at age sixty-one—no reason given) of L. R. Wright, a Canadian "much-more-than-a-mystery" writer, many of whose novels I have immensely enjoyed. She had an uncanny ability to make you feel what it might be like to have the mind and soul of a female psychopath, or to understand the circumstances and undercurrents that could lead an apparently "nice, quiet" teenage boy to explode in a murderous rage and kill his entire family. I am sad that she will write no more, especially since she was growing in power and subtlety. And I wonder how she died.

As Hopkins, always a favourite poet of Elma's, had pleaded that God send rain enough for his parched roots, so now she was pleading for hers. In the spring and summer months that led into early September, some rain fell, but never enough. She began to wonder just how she would die, just as she wondered how L. R. Wright had died. Would it be given to her to know ahead of time, or would she meet her death unprepared, like the many hundreds on that September 11th who got up for breakfast, only to fall without wings a few hours later from buildings that reached into the sky?

Elma never spoke to me directly about the tragedy in New York, but like everyone else, she must have thought about it. Life's bargain is that we die, of course. Everyone knows that, but when? how? where? Can we ever be ready? Howsoever our deaths happen, will our final moments be the same whooshing fall into nothingness, observed by those left to watch? Elma had become aware that terrorists also attack from within, and the war being waged inside her body must have been as devastating to her as the towers' collapse.

It was a friend who reminded me that Jane Austen never mentioned the "troubles" of the world beyond her characters' lives, and it's just as well. They were internalized and played out unbidden. Carol would have known and understood that. In addition to her vast creative output, she had written the biography *Jane Austen*, which won the important Charles Taylor Prize for Literary Non-Fiction.

The question of dying rarely bothers the young, when the prospect is mere theory, but facing it later, in sickness or old age, one prays not to flail or not to be seen to flail. Let others come to clear the site and build a monument.

———

Ever the realist, Elma began now seriously to contemplate her own dying and what the consequences would be for her family, her friends, and her work. For more than twenty years she had worked for literacy groups in Manitoba, first as a volunteer tutor, then a fundraiser, a writer of grant proposals, and an organizer of workshops. (Could anyone have been better qualified to show others the joy and value of reading?) Tireless in this, that fall she was recognized with a Canada Post Literacy Award as one of Canada's top five educators in the adult literacy field. The ceremony was held just three days after she learned she had terminal cancer and had announced her retirement, though no one knew why. In a picture of her with Martin, her husband, taken that night, she is seen flashing a smile so dazzling you would think she had just been granted a vision of the beyond. Maybe she had.

By late autumn, however, Elma's situation had worsened. Hopes were raised by one set of tests, dashed by another, and debilitating radiation treatments and chemotherapy sessions were ordered. The lung cancer, diagnosed that September, was beginning to spread to the brain.

Her next letter, in November, was addressed specifically to Carol, though I was co-recipient.

Responding to what Carol must have said privately about her own treatments, Elma wanted to know more. Her rational scientific mind managed always to surprise me, for she could talk about and analyze her own distresses as though they were someone else's, even when I was aware of the pain and fear she was feeling.

Dear Carol,

I'm always thinking of you, and what's been happening. I wonder if you have been on a chemo treatment called Etoposide (also called VP-16 and Vepesid)? This one makes me so susceptible to infection the whole time I am on it, which will be to the end of January, at least, if I live that long. I take it by IV at the hospital for almost a whole day, three days in a row in a month, and it has to be "flushed" constantly, day and night for three days, and I'm lucky if I can doze for even ten minutes before it's "up again, girl!" Not only does this deprive me of three days, I am often too tired to want to see anybody for a couple more. So there goes almost a week out of each month.

I still have to be very careful of balance, since that was the really big part of my brain affected. There are possible emergency treatments for this spot, but in general they avoid messing with the brain again for at least a year. Sooo—given the six months prognosis, and the brain's involvement, I'm working to a tight schedule right now. Martin says he'll kill me if I use "window of opportunity" or something similar one more time. He thinks I'm into enough windows on the computer!

Would you be willing to tell me something about the chemo you've had/are regularly having? I've always been fascinated by medicine and would, I think, have been a doctor myself if I hadn't wanted kids. Besides, I was lacking in the necessary stamina, and those were different times, eh?

There's an anecdote I'd like to share with you and A. I have always believed in something, if only that "good" and "god" are basically interchangeable terms, and have zero to do with a god who has any involvement in this world, even an impersonal one. Definitely

I think there is "a power greater than myself" as they say in AA (and even there you can use alcohol as the power, if that's all you can manage).

But do I love arguing both sides of anything! Well, my grandson Andrew had asked his parents about cancer, dying, etc. I later got him alone, with dad John off to one side, and asked if he had any more questions for me. "Yes, actually I do."

First he asked about the effects of radiation. Second he asked, "What gender are your doctors?" Even John's eyebrows went up at that one. I said so far one male and the rest female, and he said, "That's about what I figured." This is a kid who had to be rushed to emergency with asthma from infancy, so a medical interest is natural.

But he had one more question: "Do you believe God always existed?"

I said, "Basically, yes," not feeling either of us was really ready at that point for a debate on the meanings of God, existence, or the nature of the space-time continuum.

But he went on: "So you are a believer?" (No further specification.)

I said, "Yes."

He said, "Well, that's what really matters," to which I replied, "You are bang on, it is indeed."

My minister brother later remarked that Andrew had accomplished the feat of pushing me off my fence-sitting (and onto the unexpected side of the fence) after five hundred people had spent over fifty years trying to do just that!

But I find that I do have indeed a newfound faith in a God, which I still have to fight to hold to, of course. It's all bound up with the patterns within patterns, and designs within designs, I see and delight in—from the inconceivably cosmic to the tiniest grain. And it has been a great comfort and a help— in many ways. For example, it has made it so much easier to tell those with a religious belief about my dying.

And that is way more than enough for now, guys!

Carol, I love you.

A.

—ever . . . ever . . . ever . . .

E.

P.S. Carol, I want to read your new novel.

A., I want to read yours. And I'd like to read Alice Munro's latest. People naturally think "Elma + free time = reading." (Even without the free time, that's always been true.) And with the kindest intentions, I am being snowed under. I don't want more books. I want contact with old friends (and some new) right now, and that means, when I do feel like reading, it's old book-friends I choose. What so many people don't realize is that it takes energy to read—sheer eye energy, too, and my vision is very unpredictable. A couple of weeks ago, I couldn't begin to follow a plot line. People who have been sick in hospital understand this best. I'm improving a lot, thank God, but it still varies, and I have enough books to last me 99 years as it is.

To all of this Carol responded:

Dear Elma and A.,

I agree with you about reading—it is a great comfort, but often hard work. Being with friends or family is more and more what satisfies. Novels do get me out of my own consciousness, a good thing, and the best thing about novels is knowing how other people think—this means that only certain novels work.

You asked about my treatment. I am officially in palliative care, though I'm having a small dinner party tonight—hard to imagine. Among our guests is Marsha Hanen, who used to be president of the University of Winnipeg: you may know her. She suffered from lymphoma four years ago which was treated by stem cell implants, and has done well. Her friendship has been a gift. She is a thoroughly good woman. So I'm off to put the chicken in the oven, my daughter Anne's recipe. Marsha is bringing dessert. A retired engineering prof (a neighbour) from

Waterloo is coming with his "girl" friend.
This is called LIFE GOING ON.

What do you do in the middle of the
night? Is there anything to watch on TV? I
don't find TV much use at any time, though
I love CBC radio. Dear Elma—I'm thinking
of you every day.
carol

(In e-mails Carol never signed her own name with a
capital *c*.)

I noticed it was All Saints Day when Elma and
Carol wrote these letters, and I remembered that
my mother had been buried on All Saints Day,
some ten years earlier and just four years short of
her one-hundredth birthday. "Why did Daddy have
to die so young?" was her question after my father's
death. "Well, Mother," I replied, "you must remember he was ninety-two."

I am left to wonder if life is always too long or
never long enough.

Would we view life and death differently if we
believed that all we simply are is music, a collection

of vibrating strings? The friend and former student, Stephen Haff, who had reminded me about Jane Austen told me of another belief, founded on quantum physics and known as string theory, which is that everything in the universe is music. "Take one of these little strings," he told me, "flatten it with a rolling pin, keep on flattening it until you get a vast and very thin membrane. That membrane is the surface on which our universe sits, like tomato sauce on a great lasagna noodle. So the tiniest particle, the angel's hair noodle, when severely attenuated, is also the thing that contains everything."

What Elma and Carol were to write to each other and to me in the months that lay ahead would be, according to my friend, like a vast sheet of lasagna, embodying a dazzling cosmic truth. They would have appreciated such a homely analogy.

"Patterns within patterns, and designs within designs, I see and delight in—from the inconceivably cosmic to the tiniest grain," Elma had written, perceiving one of the fundamentals in creation. It's an insight ignored by right-wing religious fundamentalists and any limited scientists who aim to reduce all to a flat oneness and sameness. Famed though it is, Cleopatra's "infinite variety," as Shakespeare described the range of that Egyptian queen's seductive powers, can be thought limited only when measured against that found in plants and insects and animals and creatures that fly. Consider the complex patterns in the wings of hummingbirds, the colours in a peacock, the precise and detailed petals of any flower seen under a microscope, nothing ever exactly duplicated throughout creation. In a world of such staggering variety and abundance, Elma had also made it clear to me, in a letter written years earlier, that sexual diversity was part of the design. To her it was an obvious and accepted truth, and her earlier remark (never elaborated on) that "nature" probably "intended" her to be bisexual is best understood in such a context. God's capacity is greater than man's understanding.

And there is Carol herself, in her reply to Elma, saying almost casually that "the best thing about novels is knowing how other people think." Yes, of course, though it took her to put it that way. Plot, dialogue, arresting language, characters beyond those we might meet in everyday life, these are elements in a novel, but the key ingredient is thought. What did Daisy Goodwill think in *The Stone Diaries?* And Reta

Winters in *Unless,* what did she think? Carol has told us. And if she had ever put Elma in a novel, we would know, in this instance, what Elma thought about patterns within patterns and designs within designs.

═══

Dear Carol,

I have been mentally composing long letters to you—sorry ESP doesn't work better. Usually I can write, but not always—I've had a lot of sleep deprivation recently. Flushing out the kidneys when on chemo is necessary, I guess, but a damn nuisance!

I had my rad. marks put on yesterday, and my first session today. (Took ten minutes—no immediate side effects, except some fatigue for the rest of the day.) Last week, I had chemo Monday, Tuesday, and Wednesday from 8:30 a.m. to around 3 p.m. And I AM NOT A MORNING PERSON!

My bladder has never been that big! I don't have incontinence, but having kids has its effects, as you well know, and I've actually had four of them. One was stillborn—rubella, they said, though from what I know now I could have killed it—*him*, "Joseph Paul"— myself with a few drinks too many, though I was able to control my alcoholism during pregnancy. It's about time I started grieving for him, instead of denying his existence.

Wording her sentence precisely, in this letter to Carol she named the fetus, almost accusing herself of murder, a further torment. Shades of Hopkins again:

With this tormented mind tormenting yet
I cast for comfort I can no more get
By groping round my comfortless, than blind
Eyes in their dark can day or thirst can find
Thirst's all-in-all in all a world of wet.

It was only much later and after Elma's own death that Martin told me the doctor had been "absolutely furious" when she had refused an abortion in the second month of her pregnancy, when she knew she had rubella (German measles). Despite learning that the baby, if ever born, would be almost certainly deaf or blind or have serious heart damage, she insisted that life was important and she would try to carry the fetus to term. It was in the sixth month that the baby was stillborn, and the doctors thought seriously brain damaged. Although rubella was really the cause, Elma blamed herself. She had cut down on her drinking during pregnancy, but she now returned to alcohol in a yet more serious way and went spinning out of control. It was, however—so Martin told me later—because she recognized her own desperate situation that she started going to AA, and that led to her subsequent recovery. "The mind is its own place, and in itself can make a Heav'n of Hell, a Hell of Heav'n." True enough, even when Milton gave the words to Satan. It's the transforming mind that counts, and Elma's mind was still capable of working, still transforming.

So sleep really has been my major concern. But perhaps I should be less interested in being unconscious! I am now beginning to realize that, in my case, that "miraculous 1%" (inexplicable cure) translates into a very slim chance of living more than about six months. And with no way of knowing at all when

which or all of my mental faculties will go
during that time frame, I must try to develop
at least one new thing a day, rather than being
concerned about sleep.

I am a very happy woman, Carol, and bless
you and all my incredibly supportive friends.

Talking is usually much easier for me, but
I don't want to interrupt your work.

Read about *Unless*. Great title. That story
was the first I read in *Dressing Up for the
Carnival,* and remains one of my favourites.
I'm delighted you're picking up that one—
hope to get to read the book.

All love,

Elma

P.S. I meant *this* week I had chemo Monday,
etc., so I've had five straight days of chemo and
then rad. stuff. See what I mean about sleep?

The next day I responded to Elma's letter to Carol.

Dear E.,

Last night I got what you had addressed to
Carol and perfectly well understood. How

sensible you are becoming! Save your energies! Write only what you want and when you want to write it.

Who was it who said—Arthur Koestler got it from someone else, I think—something about the best inspirations coming from the bus, the bath, and the bed? I hope that's true, because in my morning bath a few minutes ago, I thought I should try, after all, to turn my Salvation Army novel into a play, which is what you suggested, and I even thought of an opening scene. The challenge would be to find a different way of telling the same story and not be reluctant to let go great chunks of the novel that won't fit a format for the stage. If I ever do that, I'll dedicate it to you—"For Elma, the brightest and best."

Ever . . . ever . . . ever . . .

A.

A few days later, I wrote again to Elma, knowing that she had been suffering regularly from insomnia and had asked Carol what her remedy was for getting to sleep at night. Carol's answer was unfortunately lost in a later computer glitch, but it was so vivid and imaginative that I recall it clearly.

Carol wrote that she would imagine herself standing at the top of a staircase, with as many stairs on it as there were years in her life. Sometimes it was a grand staircase, made of Italian marble, with banisters stylishly shaped and decorated with pieces of glass from Murano; sometimes it was humbler and made of wood or polished ebony; sometimes it was built of concrete, hard, durable. And, lying in bed with her eyes closed, she would start on the top step, a beginning that was also an ending.

She would descend that staircase very slowly, each step a review of her life, stopping to feel each stair with her foot, appreciating its smoothness, its colour, and looking to see if it reflected light or not, if it had been created by an obviously loving craftsman. Down, down, down, always slowly down. Sometimes she would pretend that the steps she walked on were encrusted with jewels and highly polished. Sometimes they would be of silver or gold. And as she stepped down, one by one, she would marvel at the work, its design, its symmetry, its sheer beauty, its honesty of purpose. She would continue down the staircase of her years, the journey of her life, until she found herself regressing into young adulthood by stair thirty-one, then childhood by stair twelve, but losing track of whatever number it was in infancy, where sleep never failed to arrive.

Dear E. and C.,

I have just returned from a concert in Antigonish—that name, by the way, according to guide books, is a Mi'kmaq word meaning "The place where bears gather in the winter and eat beech nuts," demonstrating an economy of language unrivalled by anything in English.

Thank you for all you have both sent. My heart is in the right place, I hope, but what the two of you are experiencing leaves me feeling helpless on the outside, even when I'm not.

I like the idea of feeling one's way down a flight of stairs in order to find sleep, and must try it sometime without falling. Do you remember, Elma, your own fall down the stairs

in my Lennoxville house long years ago? You
had brought Martin, your new husband, whom
I had not met, to stay with my wife and me in
our rented campus house, only to have me take
you to the hospital later that evening, when
you tried to stumble up the stairs to bed but fell
so badly to the bottom. More and more, however, I feel like a doctor out of Chekhov,
amazed at all he once knew and no longer
remembers in detail. Lucky for you, maybe!

I was sorting through some of my old
poems the other day, prior to reading a few at
a gathering here in Sackville, and thought you
both might like the one I will now copy out for
you, especially since it is short. (It would be
even shorter, of course, if I had a complete
vocabulary of Mi'kmaq words.) You might have
to read between the lines a bit to see that the Old
and the New Testaments are there, as well as all
those of us who search for love, everything from
one bite of apple! It was published once in a
small literary journal out of Halifax, called *The
Pottersfield Portfolio*. Its title is "Eden":

Love came from chaos at the first,
the Word transforming dark to light,
and Eve was flashed into knowing
Genesis was no myth.

One bite and the world sang its pain,
its paean of lost and found and lost again,
and Mary's flesh discovered
the tree was no myth.

But who would put the apple back?
Not I, standing at last with you,
my world held now in shining hands,
my love no myth.

Ever . . . ever . . . ever . . .

A.

I have to admit to feelings of inadequacy, as I struggled to say anything even remotely helpful to two women who were dying of cancer when I was perfectly healthy and enjoying my life. Forty years earlier, in any parallel situation, I would have felt even more inadequate. To an outsider, I would have appeared a happy man, married with two beautiful children, a son and a daughter, enjoying my work, enjoying much of my life. But I was leading parts of my life secretly, forever fearful that a disapproving world would break in and try to destroy what was there. If any two friends had told me in those bigoted, uncertain days that they were living with cancer and writing to each other about it and would I join in, I would have been at even more of a loss to say anything helpful about living and loving and dying, when so much of my own emotional energy was spent in a search to discover myself and to understand a little of what I think I understand better now.

When old age does not bring further stupidity, it can at least bring clearer perspective; for I have lived, since my divorce, in a long and settled relationship with my much younger partner, Alasdair MacLean, an established classical composer. I like to believe that even now, in my eighties, I might go on growing into more of who I am.

Dear E.,
Alasdair is now in Newfoundland, and I go there this next weekend to join him for a couple of days. So, I think of him far away, and I think

of you far away, and I think of Carol far away; but, of course, none of that is true, because none of you is far away. Don't you feel increasingly that what you carry within is far more important than what may be happening to you in some more obvious outside world?

Last night I went to hear a talk given by Sister Elaine MacInnes, Canadian born, who began a career in music (violinist at the Juilliard School) before she decided that all that wasn't enough, and an inner restlessness took her deeper within. She became a Roman Catholic nun, and later went to Japan where she studied Buddhism for years and eventually became a Zen master and was invested as roshi (old teacher). Years followed in the Philippines, working with prisoners, teaching them Zen, showing them how to be free, even when they were confined by concrete walls. In 1993, she was invited to be director of the Phoenix Trust in Oxford, and retired from that just two years ago when she turned seventy-five (my age!). She has the Order of Canada and has written a couple of books, one of which

I bought last night. Her talk was a bit rambling
and casual and not as gritty as I might have
liked, but I did get a sense of how remarkable a
human being she is, and I look forward now to
learning something more, by reading her book,
about how she marries Zen to Christianity.

I liked what Carol had to say about having
friends in for dinner and cooking a chicken. It
was the observation of very small things that
helped Lear back to sanity on the heath, you
will remember, so that he could ask forgive-
ness of his daughter Cordelia and say to her,
"We two alone will sing like birds in the
cage"; and so long as both you and Carol can
continue with some of life's little rituals, even
the very small ones like cooking a chicken, you
are likely to move further towards grace and
acceptance. But how little I know, when I'm
not going through what you're going through!
Please forgive my fumbling and awkwardness.
You know I think of you, both of you.

Ever . . . ever . . . ever . . .

A.

Elma insisted, of course, that her own life go on, as best it could, even when she continued to be deeply interested in the cancer that was destroying her. She was grateful for all she still had, but, as she would soon write to Carol, she wanted to make "a good death" when the time came.

Recognizing that we all must die, I wonder what "a good death" means. Is it a matter of good, better, best?

For the person dying, is it "good" to die in one's sleep, a quiet and final exhalation, "good" to die suddenly in a plane or car crash, when no goodbyes can be said to anyone, "good" to shut the door quickly, as if leaving a party, without even a thank you for inviting me? "Better" to die after a short illness, surrounded by family and friends and farewell speeches and tears, the inevitable known in advance? "Best" to die of old age, body broken but mind intact, a shining example of acceptance?

But what of those left behind? What is good, better and best for them? Dying, after all, is the last living thing we have to do, and one would hope to get it right.

John Donne, supreme among seventeenth-century metaphysical poets, dean of St. Paul's Cathedral, a great writer of sermons and obsessed with death, arranged for a painting of himself, wrapped in his winding sheet (reproduced later as a sculpted marble effigy for St. Paul's, where it can be seen to this day), to be set before him as a proper subject for viewing long before he died in 1631. It must have focused his mind wonderfully.

> *Donne and the Worm: If my soule could ask one of*
> *those Wormes which my dead body shall produce,*
> *Will you change with me? that worme would say,*
> *No; for you are like to live eternally in torment; for*
> *my part, I can live no longer than the putrid mois-*
> *ture of your body will give me leave, and therefore*
> *I will not change; nay, would the Devill himself*
> *change with a damned soule? I cannot tell.*

Neither Carol nor Elma went to the extreme of contemplating images of themselves in death, but they were learning what Tibetan monks had also to learn, which was how to "bring the mind home." When the Buddha, who had long been searching for the truth, more than two and a half thousand years ago, sat down under a tree in northern India, and stayed there all night, he achieved what he considered the final goal of human existence—enlightenment. There came then such a feeling of bliss that the earth shuddered, and no one anywhere was angry, ill, or sad. Everything had reached perfection, and all was quiet. He had brought his mind home.

Dear Carol,

Like you, I wish there *were* some way to reach systemic or metastasized tumours better and more directly! My sense of balance is certainly not what it was a month ago, and I wish they could zap that part of my brain again. But I can see why they are a little cagey about messing around in there, and I never was a well-balanced person at the best of times (in all senses).

I had a salutary experience just over a week ago, when I was totally flattened (and I mean that—I couldn't even crawl—I certainly wouldn't have cared if I had died) by a flu bug for twenty-four hours. The next day I felt much better, and realized that it is possible to survive feeling that awful and come out the other side.

I understand also how one can feel rotten without being in pain. In fact, so far, apart from basically manageable headaches, I have been virtually pain-free, amazingly. The primary lung tumour is giving me no trouble at all. What I feel is weak as a limp dishrag often, but that too varies in degree.

So far I have not had time to feel depressed. I still feel so lucky! The way people have responded to my illness astounds me. The love and thought-waves are palpable. Over and over friends say things like, "You know I really do love you, but I've never actually said those words to you, or to so many others. Why don't we tell people what we admire about them and how much they mean to us more often? We let all these chances slip by." And we do, indeed! Well, if I can at least help to impel a few others to appreciate and voice appreciation to their families and friends, then I am grateful.

I would like, if I can, to make a "good death"—to do something positive with this part of life that comes to us all. (Goodness, but I sound pompous!)

You ask what I do in the middle of the night. Now, Carol, take a look at the times of my e-mails! I am free to be the night person I always was for the first time in my life! I can also sometimes manage a bit of basic house-work, since that's my high-energy period . . . I watch TV for the weather forecast, and that's about it . . . I tape CBC broadcasts to listen to at appropriate times, and that has the advantage that I can erase whatever turns out to be a bore and go on to something else. What do YOU do at night? Are you still writing in the day?

Love,

Elma

On the same day that Elma wrote specifically to Carol, she wrote specifically to me, commenting on what I had said in my letter the day before.

Dearest A.,

Yes, of course what we carry within is what is real. You were one of the first to teach me that, though I need reminding. I am about to start reading the draft of your other novel, *What's Remembered*, by the way, and am so glad I am finally able to concentrate enough to read it properly, though I have skimmed bits already.

Stop undervaluing yourself, you wretched man! You are neither fumbling nor awkward. And if anyone knows about the importance of life's small ceremonies, it's Carol, and how they move one towards grace and acceptance. Her celebration of such ceremonies is the best thing about her writing, to my mind.

Don't put yourself down. You are one of the most important people in my life. You support me always and I love you immensely.

Ever . . . ever . . . ever . . .

E.

It was Elma's comment about Carol's celebrating life's small ceremonies that sent me back to her short stories, savouring again their insights and wisdom, vignettes that can haunt you for days. There is Wanda from the bank, for example, ill prepared for life's carnival, sent by her boss, the bank manager, to push an expensive new pram, "majestically hooded, tires like a Rolls-Royce," to his home for his new baby son, because there was no room in his Volvo to transport it there himself. Wanda, "an awkward girl with big girlish teeth and clumsy shoulders," who would obviously never have a baby of her own to push in any pram, stops her journey at one point, "leans over and reaches inside. There's no one about; no one sees her, only the eyes inside her head that have rehearsed this small gesture in dreams. She straightens the blanket, pulling it smooth, pats it into place. 'Shhh,' she murmurs, smiling. 'There, there, now.'" Who but Carol Shields could conjure up, in such a small incident and with so few words, the sad-sweet life of a lonely woman whose only joy was in imagining what she would never have?

I carried with me this awareness of Elma's love when I joined Alasdair, visiting schools in Newfoundland as composer-in-residence for Debut Atlantic, a touring organization for classical artists.

The few days away included November 11th, a day that had long held special significance for me.

Remembrance Day had always been a time for reflection, even when I was a child, growing up in Bermuda, an idyllic and peaceful place in the 1920s and '30s, when the rest of the world shuddered its own dark way from one world war into another. I first reflected seriously on death at the age of seven, when pleurisy kept me in bed for three months and out of school for one long year—those were the days before antibiotics—and I wondered then if I would live. My parents must have wondered, too, but I learned to walk again and returned to school, though not to play soccer or cricket for yet another year.

I went with my parents to the Cenotaph on Front Street in Hamilton, Bermuda's capital, every November 11th, and standing there during a long two minutes of silence, I waited to hear one particular name read out—my own, though it was that of the first Arthur Motyer, killed in a muddy field in France. A big, tall, handsome man, a Rhodes Scholar, an engineer, and my father's only brother, he had been shot by a sniper's bullet in 1916, just as he stepped out of a trench to connect a telephone wire, before an assault the next day. "A prince among men" was how his batman, writing a letter of sympathy to my grandfather in Bermuda, described the man whose name I have carried since birth, always wondering if I was meant to be someone else, though never compared with him by parents who loved me. "He died for freedom and honour" were the words on a bronze plaque engraved with his full name, ARTHUR JOHN MOTYER, sent by the government to comfort my father and grandfather, who grieved without understanding or forgiving the world's stupidity. Was his "a good death"? The plaque hangs now from a mantelpiece in my Sackville house, reminding me of a death before Elma's and Carol's, and of my own to come.

═══

Dear A. and E.,

It's good to hear from you both. Elma, I'm hoping this next chemo is accompanied by the wonderful golden (expensive and gold-coloured) anti-nausea pills. About hair:

I think I've finally realized that the hair issue
is germane only to the hair loser, though I
grieved and continue to grieve about it. It is
not vanity, but rather the integrity of the
body broken—added to all the other indignities. We have done three things this month,
and we're ticking them off. We've gone to
the Giller, gone to Calgary for convocation,
and gone to Vancouver for a PET scan
(results to come). We have one more thing to
do—leaving Sunday for Paris where my play
Thirteen Hands will open on Tuesday night.
We'll be home on Thursday and will stay in
the nest here in Victoria forever. This is
where I really want to be at the moment. I am
thinking of you every day and hoping you are
ever your bright and wise self.

    love,

carol

She rightly thought that to grieve over the loss
of one's hair should not be interpreted as vanity,
compared with the greater indignities of a body
broken. But the comment for me had special reso-

nance, for the thick head of wavy hair I had in my youth I began to lose in my twenties, and I grieved about it for years. My body, all the while, had not been broken, and I was in good health. Only now, therefore, do I realize how much vanity there was in this superficial grieving, for my only wish was to be admired. "You have the most marvellous head of hair I have ever seen on a man" was the comment I got frequently in the 1940s, and when I was seventeen, cast as the romantic lead in a university production of *Romeo and Juliet*, I let my hair grow even longer, in the hope of being admired even more.

Vanity, vanity, was the sole root of my grieving. Bald now since middle age, I might have benefited earlier from Carol's wisdom, that "the hair issue is germane only to the hair loser."

Carol had said she had done three things that month, when she was so ill: one very private (the PET scan); one more public (a university convocation); and the third, an event open to the world on television (the Giller awards in Toronto). She had not published anything that year, and was, therefore, not up for the prestigious literary award, when

Richard Wright won for *Clara Callan*. But the warm response she got from everyone present at the gala was her own personal award.

It was especially because Elma's daughter, Beth, was living in Paris when Carol wrote about going there that Elma got back to her immediately.

Dear Carol,

How wonderful that you are going to the opening of *Thirteen Hands*—at least, I hope it is wonderful for YOU, though I can well understand why you want to stay put there-after. I'll see if my daughter can get tickets and tell me all about your success.

I had the "gold pill" last time, and no nausea at all. It was the three days sitting on the toilet that got me down (or rather up).

I'm getting floods of lovely tributes from the literacy field as people gradually learn about the fact that I am not absent from events because of retirement. I must say it's nice to hear some of this *before* the funeral. A bit of basking won't hurt, I hope.

Life at the moment is golden—and if

you've been tracking the weather here, you
will know how incredible it's been.

   Love always,
Elma

More than ten days elapsed before I felt able to
make any sort of reply. Sometimes I found it truly
difficult to know what to say. How could two such
people possibly need me? What could I offer?
Words, words, words. Are they ever enough?

Dear Elma and Carol,

   I know that you, Elma, have had friends
and family with you just recently, and I hope
it has been a happy time for you. As for me,
I have been here and there with Alasdair for
these last several days, but always I have
taken you with me. Carol, you, too, I pre-
sume, are back from Paris, taking Elma with
you on that longer trip, which must have been
tiring for both of you, so get extra rest now.

   It might cheer both of you to hear that I
was at a concert last night in Rothesay, when
one of Alasdair's works was performed by

the wunderkind cellist Denise Djokic, on her
six-million-dollar Bonjour Stradivari cello,
on loan from the Canada Council. Really
stunning, both the music and the perform-
ance! At the intermission, I was introduced
to, and had a lovely long chat with, Gordon
Fairweather, a couple of years older than I
and now retired from politics, a real delight,
unpretentious, droll, and wonderfully
human. A lawyer originally, he was, in his
time, chairman of the Immigration and
Refugee Board and then the Human Rights
Commission. When I commented that, in my
career, I had met few academics who were
large, generous spirits, he smiled softly and
said that years ago he had been on a search
committee to select a new president for the
University of New Brunswick, and had never
before witnessed such vicious in-fighting as
he saw then among the professors, though he
had spent twenty-five years in the Liberal
caucus! Lester Pearson had been his
favourite prime minister and had taught him
one of life's more important lessons, which

was 'Learn to say *no*!,' though that was, unfortunately, also a line from a temperance hymn about the evils of drink!

Enough chatter for now. I think of you, both of you.

Ever . . . ever . . . ever . . .

A.

In the weeks that followed, Elma began expressing thoughts that were more sombre than when she mentioned "a bit of basking" before the funeral. It would prove a roller-coaster ride of lengthening shadows and sunshine. But lines from Hopkins would always be there:

> *I wake and feel the fell of dark, not day.*
> *What hours, O what black hours we have spent*
> *This night! what sights you, heart, saw; ways*
> *   you went!*
> *And more must, in yet longer light's delay.*

TWO

But Fay's noticed something she's never noticed before. That love is not, anywhere, taken seriously. It's not respected. It's the one thing in the world everyone wants—she's convinced of that—but for some reason people are obliged to pretend that love is trifling and foolish. . . . It's possible to speak ironically about romance, but no adult with any sense talks about love's richness and transcendence, that it actually happens, that it's happening right now, in the last years of our long, hard, lean, bitter and promiscuous century.

—From *The Republic of Love*

Dear C. and A.,

Middle of the night chills time. I was just reading the latest *Maclean's* (mistake No. 1, no doubt) and it contained a description of ex-Beatle Paul McCartney visiting George Harrison, who has entered "the final stage of his life." Apparently, George denied the existence of his "brain cancer" (as they call it—it's metastasized lung cancer, just like mine) in July, and on October 1st he recorded a sound track for an album, and now he's reached the end. That's less than two months ago.

Oh well, I was glad to see that while Paul had cried, George was in pretty good spirits. (Probably manic on steroids, unfortunate man, as my doctor accuses me of being when she thinks I'm too cheerful.) At least he appears to be somewhat compos mentis. But the speed with which a lung cancer patient can go from functioning fairly normally to being at death's door has clearly not been exaggerated. On the other hand, perhaps that's not such a bad thing . . . oh dear, I seem to be an incurable optimist.

I might add that Mart and I have been having some fairly intensive talk sessions and I think he is really going through a very bad patch right now. The reality of the situation is beginning to hit him pretty hard. Actually, I think it's just as well that he had that transition period of denial. I guess it's a phase one has to go through at some point, and I'm not sure I've quite finished with it yet myself, though I seem to be experiencing a number of the so-called requisite stages simultaneously. Anyway, I hope we can do some special things together—and with friends and family—during the next few months, and also just *be*.

And now I will go back to reading *Winnie-the-Pooh* or *The Wind in the Willows*—both, in their very different ways, extremely profound books, and of far more lasting impact than anything in *Maclean's*, thank God. Do you ever re-read those classics? Winnie has all kinds of helpful hints for cheering oneself up in scary situations, and even for hanging on for dear life (as when dangling in the air surrounded by bees).

A few days later, she wrote again, but just to me.

I am not dead—indeed, I am very well right now, and also very busy. I'm trying to do 100 things before (a) my next round of chemo beginning December 12th and (b) Christmas visitors, who start arriving December 18th—just as I'm back on my feet again, I hope!

Carol's cancer has suddenly become much more aggressive. At this point, we both realize how little time we have, but Carol has had many ups and downs, and hers will probably be a slower process, whereas right now I am in quite good shape. But when the brain starts to lose it, it will do so at quite a speed, from what I've been told.

In whatever time she and Carol had left, however, it became evident that they would both summon the strength to cope with prejudice and stupidity wherever found, sometimes even in doctors.

In early December, Elma had indicated to Carol her state of fury over a letter her doctor had written in support of a disability claim: she was critical of the letter's phrasing, its offhand tone, its lack of sensitivity. Furthermore, she found difficulty talking to Martin about it, worried that he was

still in some sort of state of denial, and we never seem to have time to talk about the things that really matter. We do not really have an easy communication system—

shorthand or otherwise—for this situation as yet. It came on us too suddenly, I think, though it has improved a great deal in the past few days, and will continue to do so, especially as Mart will be teaching only one course next term. His department head offered to have someone else take over the other.

Carol had written back the same day.

Dear Elma,

You need never apologize to me for a burst of outrage. I'm on your team here. Please continue to hold my hand, as I will hold yours, all the way.

Tactless doctors. And how dare they use the word *lady* or *ladies*. Oiiiiii! Really, a good many of them have not evolved. (I'm feeling very evolved these days, a comfort.)

Your words about Martin not being able to talk to you about this struck Don—who has always read my mail (I read his too). It's like having a joint account. Should we be talking

more? he asked me. My answer: we are talking
all the time, only in the very private code
we've evolved over all these forty-four years,
part of it gesture, of course, and certain kinds
of jokes. Neither of us knows how to do this,
but I don't want to do it the sappy way, whatever that means.

   My dear friend, hang on tight.

   love,

carol

   I felt myself challenged again for something to
say to Elma that might be of interest to Carol. I
could understand their anger about the doctor's dis-
missive tone, recognizing, as I did, that under any
civilized veneer, including my own, there lurk
always passions ready to erupt, even when triggered
by something relatively small. "We are the animals
Christ is rumoured to have died for," wrote
Robinson Jeffers, the great American poet. And
were it not for the redemptive flashes of insight
coming now from Carol and Elma, I could be easily
persuaded, in my own dark moments, that Jeffers
spoke the truth.

Thus I began one early December morning:

Good morning, dear E. and C.!

I would like to think you are both sleeping peacefully as I start this at 9 a.m. my time, but, knowing you, Elma, you are probably wide awake, while you, Carol, in Victoria, may be moving down a beautiful set of curving crystal stairs in search of sleep and finding it before you get to the bottom.

After both your letters, I am teased out of thought, contemplating all the things I don't understand and may never. I have not been afflicted like Job, like both of you, though maybe in other emotional ways, years ago, at the time of my divorce, wondering how I would survive and almost didn't. Do I deserve now to be with Alasdair on this wonderful plateau of understanding in old (or is it just older) age, and to be with other friends and family, as well, rejoicing in every day I have? No, of course I don't deserve it, any more than each one of you deserves what has been measured out to you. I cannot know, I can only imagine what it must be like to be counting the days, as you must now count them, but I suppose, also, as all of us must and should now count them. One day at a time, O Lord! "Sufficient unto the day is the evil thereof." "Consider the lilies of the field, how they grow; they toil not, neither do they spin." It has all been said already. I blather on, but my heart is full.

The "private code of communication" that you, Carol, spoke of puts it beautifully. In varying ways and to varying degrees, that's what we all share. A blunt, head-on verbal explication just won't do. Music, in its highest forms, can move us towards that other state of being. You and I, Elma, realized that a long time ago when we listened to Mahler together.

Blue jays and black-capped chickadees are now at the bird feeder below the upstairs window of my small study where I am writing this. The day advances, and you are surely now awake. I hope it will be a good day for each of you.

Ever . . . ever . . . ever . . .

A.

Elma's reply came the following day, and I wrote again two days after that.

Dear A.,

Actually, I was asleep, so there! Why wouldn't I be at 11.30 a.m. my time? It's one of my best times for sleeping. As to Carol and me, of course you too have been, and will be, afflicted with times of wondering how you will survive. You understand, and know how to express that understanding, very well indeed.

As for suffering, I endured far more and— worse—inflicted far more, and with more painful damage to everyone concerned, when I was drinking. Paradoxically, perhaps, a lot of what I learned, and have tried to make a part of my approach to life, comes from that period and from AA. Maybe it's all just a part of a much bigger picture. I hope so.

Ever . . . ever . . . ever . . .

E.

Dear E.,

I guess it was inevitable that for so many
years, as you were coping with your life and
your family and I was coping with mine, our
communication became little more than an
exchange of Christmas cards. Now, when
you write as you have just done, I feel the
great gap. But we have the present, and the
present matters. You're there. I'm here. But
I'm also there.

Ever . . . ever . . . ever . . .

A.

It was, indeed, a great gap, for I had moved my
family in 1970 from Bishop's University in Quebec
to Mount Allison in New Brunswick, and the adjust-
ment was difficult for all of us. I was caught up in
university politics as a dean and then academic vice-
president; my wife was understandably unhappy as
she tried to cover up a broken marriage; and my
children had to make new friends in a new place. But
even before my move to eastern Canada, Elma had
produced a son and a daughter, John and Beth, in
1967 and 1969, and then her stillborn son in 1971.

There had been a ten-year addiction to alcohol, and an attempt at suicide, more of a cry for help, when she had slashed her left wrist in three places with razor blades, and was kept in a hospital ward for five days—shut up against her will, as she expressed it. But soon after that, she began her long, tough journey to recovery through AA, and a perfectly healthy son, James, was born in 1973.

In our Christmas cards, there were only incomplete references made to all of these happenings, little notes that did nothing to indicate her deepest anguish, nothing to indicate mine. The nature of friendship, however, is such that gaps of time are of no real consequence, for anything truly there in the first place is never completely lost.

Elma was in better spirits when she wrote to Carol that same December day:

Dear Carol,

You asked me once about AA. Essentially, the idea is that you have to believe in a "power greater than yourself." This can be, and often is in these more secular times, the power of the group you belong to. Or a special circle of friends. It can certainly be love. (For many years, that's what it was for me.) I have known of a number of people who at least began by agreeing that alcohol was a power greater than themselves . . . but since one is also supposed to believe that this power can "restore us to sanity," I think one would eventually have to take it a bit further! So, no, one does not have to believe in God, though recently I have discovered that in fact I do, somewhat to my surprise, though I would hate to try to define the concept, since it is both infinitely cosmic and as close as my heartbeat. It's more a question of believing that there *is* something you can draw on when you need help.

One of the aims of AA is to take yourself out of the centre of the universe. And you do this by reaching out of your own experience to try to help someone else—if you don't pass it on, you lose it, so to speak. A very old and sound method of healing. I've seen it at work in psychiatric wards where far more good was done to patients by fellow patients than by any professional. It's truly amazing and wonderful to watch a person who has been sunk in total apathy and depression roused to reach out a hand to help someone even worse off. (Another valuable experience I gained from being an alcoholic—and one which I think has helped me to understand and, I hope, help others—was being shut up against my will in such a ward.)

A very happy note: I had a blood check today, and after the last awful round of chemo, my white cells are down so much and I am so anemic, that I don't have to have any more chemo until January. I get a blood transfusion next week, instead—a *much* nicer prospect. It also explains why I have been feeling so tired and draggy recently. My naps were certainly getting longer and more frequent. I was afraid it was the beginning of the end, or something.

In addition, for the next four days (I've already done one today) I get to "shoot up" with a substance that is supposed to stimulate my bone marrow into making more white cells. All this means that I will *not* barely be recovering from chemo when my family starts arriving, nor do I have to worry for the next couple of months about every little sniffle someone else may have. Not only that, but my doctor doubled my dose of dexamethasone to help restore some of my diminishing sense of physical balance and coordination—she was actually the one who suggested it!

Anyway, I feel as if I have been given a new lease on life. To say nothing of the excitement of learning how to inject myself, albeit only subcutaneously so far. You never know when a skill like that will come in handy!

Much love,

Elma

On my birthday that year, without even realizing it was my birthday, Elma sent me the sort of present that makes any teacher's life worthwhile, fulfilling her own injunction to express what is truly in the heart while one is still alive to express it. "Why don't we tell people what we admire about them and how much they mean to us more often? We let all these chances slip by," she had earlier written to Carol, passing on what friends had suggested all of us should do.

Dear A,

This is a somewhat belated reply to something you said earlier about the years during which we were mainly in touch through Christmas cards. Well, yes . . . in a literal and detailed sense. But when have we ever really been out of touch?

Never forget that, since I was seventeen years old, you have been one of the people who has most influenced my life, and always been one of the most important people in it. You taught me so much about truly seeing and hearing—not just in literature and especially in drama, but in life—about sensitivity to other people and attitudes, about taking the time to care. I can't think of a way you ever influenced me but for good. You made me a better person than I would have been without knowing you.

No, I don't mean you're perfect, and I didn't put you on a pedestal even when I was an undergrad. You were, for example, a *most* irritating person to work with sometimes on a play, when you said things like—"Well, I don't care how you get the effect, with or without make-up. I know she's a healthy twenty-year-old, but she has to look as if she's fifty and dying of syphilis. That's *your* problem—just *do* it." And I did, eventually!

And your understanding was always there, as I hope you know mine was for you, without words, and over whatever time and distance. You said it yourself: "You're there. I'm here. But I'm also there." And will be.

Ever . . . ever . . . ever . . .

E.

Knowing that I took time to care, back when we were both young, may have been what led Elma to entrust herself to me, as she did for all those last months of her life. But how do I account for the caring? Was my caring intuitive or premeditated? I should like to think the first, but something of the second was also mixed in, the result of a personal experience when I was a student at Oxford.

In my final set of critical exams, I did badly, and this after my tutor thought I would do particularly well. "I have great hopes you'll get a good degree," said this distinguished scholar, with whom I had been working once a week for two years. Whether it was on the Scottish Chaucerians or *Tristram Shandy* or the use made by Shakespeare of Holinshed's *Chronicles* when writing the history plays, I was made to cover every possible topic in the great sweep of English literature, starting with *Beowulf*, reading it in Anglo-Saxon, and ending with the Victorians. It was just the two of us in his college study, the ideal way for anyone to learn, with the great man assuring me at the end of two years that I would get a "good" degree, by which he meant first-class honours or a "good second." But when that did not happen, I was unable to tell him why or explain the results to any-one else. I thought him on an intellectual plane so far above me that he could never have understood my inner turmoil. Besides, I was afraid. Between my own heart and mind, there had occurred a total split.

The lingering effects of whooping cough were

still with me—a serious enough affliction when one is an adult—but beyond that, I was emotionally and intellectually devastated from an unreciprocated love affair that I could tell no one about, because it was with another man. Neither was I later comforted to know that A. E. Housman had suffered much the same academic fate at Cambridge years before, and for much the same reason—and it wasn't whooping cough. The story is there in *A Shropshire Lad:*

> *Oh, when I was in love with you,*
> *   Then I was clean and brave,*
> *And miles around the wonder grew*
> *   How well I did behave.*

> *And now the fancy passes by,*
> *   And nothing will remain,*
> *And miles around they'll say that I*
> *   Am quite myself again.*

That was 1896. Fifty years later, being gay was still a criminal offence, and I saw no way to climb out of my despair.

Somehow I survived, but only just. Crossing

back to Canada by ship some weeks later, I seriously contemplated jumping into the dark Atlantic; and that image of myself standing at the rail, looking down into a black ocean, remains terrifying. But I made then a vow that I would try to care as deeply as I could for any student I might eventually have, if I ever became a teacher. I would try for the caring instead of the detachment I felt from those higher up when I was a student in crisis. In that way, I might, at least, redress a balance. Patterns within patterns. Designs within designs. I would do what I could. Elma, in time, became part of that pattern.

———

It was shortly after my mid-December birthday that Carol initiated a philosophic pre-Christmas discussion with Elma on the nature of happiness. It was timed for the season. No matter the circumstances, doesn't everyone want to be happy?

Dear E.,

My daughter Anne was here for two days this week, and I asked her if she had any advice for me. "Be happy," she said. This made us both laugh because we used to make fun of *Reader's Digest* articles about "Being Happy While Dying of Cancer." But it does, in a way, seem a choice we can make. Do you agree or not? Why would we waste precious time being unhappy? But it may be we have no control over this. I think of you every day.

much love,

carol

Dear C.,

Your apparently simple question about choosing to be happy set off a great debate between me and my cousin (whose brother died of cancer last year), and later with another friend whose husband died in September of the same kind of cancer I have, and who has the same way of handling life's vicissitudes—i.e., usually with a black sense of humour. We ranged all over the map from the existence (or not) of free will, to the nature of hedonism (a very hard philosophical position to refute)— i.e., that if you choose to be miserable, you are doing so because being miserable makes you happy, so you are always choosing to be happy, no matter what.

I have known a woman, and you have probably known someone like her, who made the worst of every possible situation, and apparently enjoyed every minute of it. Nothing was ever to her satisfaction: there was always a "Yes, but if only you/she/he had . . ." Of course she made other people miserable, too, (her children felt guilty when she died because they were really *not* sorry) and seemed to take great satisfaction in doing so.

Love always,

Elma

Provoked by this exchange, I began asking myself the age-old questions that defy easy answers. What is the true nature of happiness? How can we reach it and hold it? Should it even be the ultimate goal? Is anything more important? Is it only a selfish state of being, achieved always at the expense of others? Does every definition of happiness cancel out another? "Even a happy life," Carl Jung wrote, "cannot be without a measure of darkness, and the word 'happy' would lose its meaning if it were not balanced by sadness."

From Aristotle to Marx, from the Beatitudes of Christ to the words of Saint Augustine, and on to Bobby McFerrin with his catchy little song, "Don't Worry, Be Happy," everyone has said something about what is, after all, a private state of being. "Happiness cannot come from without," said Helen Keller. "It must come from within."

It was then I thought to ask my friend Dean Brinton for his views. He had worked with Carol on the Canada Council a few years earlier, and with his background in philosophy and arts management, I knew he would send a thoughtful reply. When it came, I forwarded it to Carol and Elma.

Dear Arthur,

While it all seems terribly grim to wonder whether happiness can or should be possible while dying, it well may be a choice we can make. (It was Abraham Lincoln who claimed that "most folks are about as happy as they make up their minds to be," but I doubt that

he would have included the terminally ill.)
But is it?

I've often wondered whether one might
achieve true happiness by following simple
prescriptions, much in the way that Pascal
thought a non-believer might become a
Christian—go to church, sing, pray if you
can. While it may be possible to will oneself to
be agreeable, to "look as well as one can, dress
as becomingly as possible, talk low, act courte-
ously, be liberal with praise, criticize not at all,
nor find fault with anything and not try to
regulate or improve anyone," happiness is
thought to be quite another matter.

But is it really? Maybe a few months of
being agreeable would lead to quite an exqui-
site form of happiness (having never been
agreeable for more than a few hours at a time,
I wouldn't know). Now if we were also to
spend a little time every day thinking of God,
we might be happy Christians too!

Do you remember the Louis Malle film
from the early '80s titled *My Dinner with
Andre*? Quite a treatise on happiness. I had

forgotten all about it until just before Christmas when I opened a fortune cookie in Montreal—"You see beauty in simple things. Do not lose this ability." Family, friends, things in nature—what more do we need? But we've come to expect so much more.

I will always keep our home on St. Margaret's Bay in Nova Scotia as a constant (lots of birds, pine trees, and water, most importantly a feeling of contentment whenever I'm there) even as I feel compelled to see how much I can get away with in the wider world. This latter motivation is a marvel for me. I'm never sure if I really want to make a contribution of one sort or another or if it's blind ambition, any more than a miserable person is aware that their misery is for them a form of happiness.

What you might expect often turns out to be the opposite. The saintly Mother Teresa, after all, was narcissistic, and, towards the end of her life, expressed grave doubts about the existence of God. At the other end of the scale, the randy British philosopher A. J. Ayer—he expressed his atheism at every opportunity throughout his career—saw a bright light while undergoing heart surgery in his eighties, though he later claimed it only "slightly weakened" his conviction that death is truly the end of everything.

So be happy if you can, and if you can't, as Kurt Vonnegut Jr. put it best, "So it goes." And so it goes with me.

Love,
Dean

After reading Dean's reflections, I realized that what Carlyle had written in *Past and Present* was near my own view. For him, in 1843, the awareness that one had been blessed was more important than any feeling of ephemeral happiness.

Does not the whole wretchedness, the whole *Atheism* as I call it, of man's ways, in these generations, shadow itself for us in that unspeakable Life-philosophy of his: the pretension to be what he calls "happy"? Every pitifulest whipster that walks within a skin has his head filled with the notion that he is, shall be, or by all human and divine laws ought to be, "happy" . . ."Happy," my brother? First of all, what difference is it whether thou art happy or not! Today becomes Yesterday so fast, all Tomorrows become Yesterdays; and then there is no question whatever of the "happiness," but quite another question.

Earthly experiences can make most of us happy—good food, good music, good sex, having our basic needs met, driving a reliable car, being physically fit, growing a rare blue Himalayan poppy, all such things and more on an endless list—but unless a deep inner sense of continued well-being comes as a blessed result, that happiness can only be shallow and fleeting. Sitting contemplatively under a tree, however, in search of enlightenment, may bring a deep inner happiness, just as climbing a mountain to discover the truth of the Beatitudes may bring a lasting joy. Being happy and being blessed can then become fused.

Elma wrote again the next day, bearing good news:

Dear A.,

On a note of serendipity—last summer, I wrote a letter of appreciation to Eleanor Wachtel, thanking her for the many hours of pleasure she has given me, and now she has sent me a copy of her book *More Writers and Company,* which contains a long section on Carol. Gee—if only I could arrange for that fate to befall my letters at will, I could build up quite a library!

I saw my radiologist today, and although of course she can give me no predictions, etc., she seems very happy with the symptomatic results of the brain radiation (i.e., I can walk and talk, I guess!). What she said was, "Get back to me when you develop a problem—you're too good for me now."

Ever . . . ever . . . ever . . .

E.

Dear E,

Good news from your radiologist: why shouldn't you be the one to defy all the odds?

"Be happy!" as Carol's daughter says.

Ever . . . ever . . . ever . . .

A.

Almost two years after Carol's diagnosis, Eleanor Wachtel conducted the beautifully sensitive interview, aired first on CBC Radio on February 27, 2000, and later included in *More Writers and Company*. What Carol had so openly said in that interview about living with cancer must have got through to Elma in some personal way, binding her yet more closely to Carol.

Carol had admitted to Eleanor she could hardly breathe from the shock she had felt at first, and how an air of unreality had accompanied the shock. She had "very naively thought [she] was not the breast cancer type"; but recognizing that she "couldn't turn it back," she had gone on to accept it, surprised at how good people were to her, even as she had to face some loss of her self-sovereignty. To be in touch with others, however, had been extremely helpful: she "needed so badly the experience of other people so that you don't feel so alone in that sorrow." In order to enlarge her world, she read more novels than she was in the habit of doing, and hoped to find some that were funny, because "life is very rich in comedy."

Carol looked for the same thing that Charles Darwin looked for when he got members of his family to read a novel to him in the afternoon, after he had done his scientific work in the morning, in the hope of finding a person he could love. Carol herself needed to escape the terrible introspection that accompanied any diagnosis of cancer. She could now see it as "a natural rhythm in your life," though it also made her "more conscious of mortality."

No wonder Eleanor Wachtel spoke later of Carol's "particular kind of humanity . . . the foundation of her commitment to writing as a form of redemption." And no wonder Carol and Elma had bonded as they did.

The happiness I had urged upon Elma was all too soon turned into something more like resignation when, just three days before Christmas, she wrote to tell Carol and me of the death from cancer of one of their mutual friends in Winnipeg.

Dear A.,

This is about the death yesterday of our friend Lynn McLean, who battled incredibly heroically for about fifteen years against what began as breast cancer. Her remissions and reprieves were simply off any known medical charts, but she had many other problems which developed over the years. She was ultimately on home dialysis, and during the last year had suffered from a terrible clinical depression. Her husband, Murdith, who teaches with Martin in the philosophy department, is, of course, anguished, but I think it will be a relief, ultimately, as it will be for her two children, and the grandchildren whose Nana, as they knew her, had all but vanished.

Ever . . . ever . . . ever . . .

E.

Dear Carol,

Murdith phoned us this morning, and he said he was going to e-mail you. He sounded very accepting, and he probably told you that the whole family was able to be there at the end, at the Palliative Care Ward at St. Boniface, when she just quietly stopped breathing.

I am very glad she is finally at peace, after these last months especially. There is nothing more to say, really.

But the circle somehow seems to stay unbroken.

Much love,
Elma

Dear Elma,

Yes, the circle does seem unbroken. I've relived a series of memories since hearing from you, once dropping in on Lynn and Murdith in the evening. She was rather sleepy, and said, "Murdith was just brushing my hair." What an amazing image. It has been such a long struggle, and I half-know what people mean when they say 'being at peace.'

much love,

c.

Christmas in Sackville that year for Alasdair and me happened to be quieter than usual, without house guests, and I sent two lines on Christmas Eve to let Elma know I was thinking of her. When we held our traditional Boxing Day lunch for a number of friends, first singing carols around the piano, drinking rum eggnog, and then eating Bermuda cassava pie—a native dish introduced from the West Indies, with a filling of chicken and veal contained in a sweet and nutmeg-spicy pudding-like crust made from the grated root of cassava—I yet wondered how Elma was coping with Lynn's death in Winnipeg.

The children and grandchildren were home. Santa Claus would come. Life had to go on. Her son James had just got engaged. They would all have dinner, but no cassava pie. They might even sing. But Christmas for her would never happen again. She must have known that. "Falls the shadow. For thine is the kingdom . . . This is the way the world ends . . . This is the way the world ends . . ." T. S. Eliot now in her head, and the Magi:

A cold coming we had of it,
Just the worst time of the year
For a journey, and such a long journey:
The ways deep and the weather sharp,
The very dead of winter.

Everyman had said it already: "I am to go a journey, a long way, hard and dangerous." She knew that.

Make the most of it.

Be happy.

And she was.

Shortly before Christmas, her radiologist had said, "Get back to me when you develop a problem. You're too good for me now." So instead of singing "Fails my heart I know not how / I can go no longer," she had done the opposite: she had gone boldly on with her family. "Thanks in part to having no chemo to deal with, I have had a fair bit of energy and the whole visit has gone *very* well," she wrote, after the children had left.

It was all "poignantly beautiful," Martin told me later, and everyone had a great time. But even with all this personal happiness, Elma had vowed that "barring unforeseen disasters," she would go to Lynn's funeral two days after Christmas. She described it to Carol early in the New Year.

Dear Carol,

There were a great number of people at Lynn McLean's funeral on the 27th. The Anglican service is always rather cold and formal, to my Anglican-raised way of thinking, and I have come to prefer a memorial service where people speak more informally. But it was moving all the same.

For me, it was also kind of eerie. For one thing, I was wearing the same pants I wore at Beth's wedding, and had once more to walk (wobble?) up a very long aisle (in order to take communion), divided by a casket instead of a font this time. Also, all the McLean clan were in plaids and kilts, as the Scots and our own family had been for the wedding.

The other strange thing was that it gave me almost a "dress-rehearsal" feeling. Virtually everyone there was connected with the philosophy department or St. John's

College, so they all were aware of my situation.

The closing hymn was "Morning Has Broken," with which I was not very familiar, but as hymns go, it's rather lovely. The melody is an old Gaelic air, and adds a great deal. It's definitely Lynn.

Carol, I send you love as always, and wish you peace, and rest for tired eyes, tired mind, tired body—whatever needs it most. And I wish you sunlit grass, and the vision of each day as a new creation.

Elma

Dear Elma,

Thank you so much for letting us know what Lynn's service was like: I do love "Morning Has Broken," and it does sound like Lynn. Yes, we too have found the St. George's services somewhat cold, without the voice of the one who has gone. And yes, I do know what you mean by the strange sense of "dress rehearsal."

All "this" has made my usual rejoicing in

the new year, new resolutions, new projects,
quite different, and so I did, as you suspected,
finish the holiday with a sense of exhaustion
and not much clarity. (I asked Don, one morning when I was overwhelmed, whether I had to
pay attention to the situation in Argentina, and
he said No.)

Random House is sending you (probably
already have) a galley of *Unless*, as you
requested. Please don't ever hesitate to write.
It is important to feel I have a partner in
"this." Going along and sharing insights.

I am about to go off with my daughter Sara
for her birthday lunch. She is thirty-four
today. I will write more later.

Much love, dear friend,
carol

In Carol's short bracketed question about
Argentina and the answer Don gave her lies one of
life's great truths, beautifully and simply expressed; for
while we are challenged always to take a larger vision
of the world, we have ultimately to live in the place
where we are, and deal with everything there, rather

than be anxious about what more we might do elsewhere. Don was right in his counselling: Carol's contribution to a suffering world was already big enough.

The next day, I added for Elma something of a postscript, which brought to mind also Mahler's *Das Lied von der Erde,* which tells how the lovely earth in spring grows green again.

> Dear E.,
> Remember Strindberg's *A Dream Play,* in which the daughter of the god Indra is sent to earth to assess mankind's predicament? "Go down and see," says Indra. "Truly a discontented, thankless race is this of earth . . . Descend and see and hear, then come again and tell me if their lamentations and complaints are justified." And after every encounter with a variety of human situations, the daughter's report to her father is always the same: "Human beings are to be pitied." But we might also remember what the daughter said at the beginning of the play: "I see that earth is fair . . . It has green woods, blue waters, white mountains, yellow fields."

Ever . . . ever . . . ever . . .

A.

Getting things right, putting things straight, while still alive to do that, was one of Elma's concerns, which is why she mentioned the Rodgers and Hammerstein musical *Carousel* in her reply. She might not have seen the Stratford production in 1997, but she had obviously thought about how best to use one's time on earth.

Dear A,

I don't know the Strindberg play you refer to, but I like the image of the earth: I just hope we don't screw that up as well. I was also reminded of *Carousel*. As you may remember, Billy, who gets killed in a bank robbery when desperate for money, has a chance to return to earth for a day to do one good deed, which he eventually does, though his first reaction is not even to look at the daughter he never saw in life.

I think my lot will do OK eventually—when I think how long it took to get things right between Mart and me . . . At least there is a lot of love there—of that I have no doubts. And it took a wee while for you to orient your own love life, *n'est ce pas?*

Ever . . . ever . . . ever . . .

E.

How rhetorically but genuinely innocent was this last little sentence of Elma's, punctuated with a French question! Innocent as a purling stream can still bring with it, from dark and forbidding mountains of memory, the sludge of years. For me, it brought the layers of pain from a broken marriage, the anxieties of concealment, the failures to my truthful self, and the sorrows of an adversarial divorce, until all was carried away and allowed to sink into an ocean of unrecoverable loss. Only then was I able to venture onto a greater sea of sunlight and love.

Elma knew the whole story, as I knew hers. She was right. It had just taken a wee while, n'est ce pas? What I had not been able to tell my Oxford tutor, I had been able to tell her.

In the week following, because Elma had found many references, always favourable, to bees in Carol's stories, she had asked her about them. Strangely enough, the prescient references predated Carol's cancer.

Dear Elma,

About bees: did I send you my favourite poem by the late Karl Shapiro? Faced with death, he compared himself to a cut flower rather than a flower with roots, and the poem ends like this:

Yesterday I was well, and then the gleam,
The thing sharper than frost cut me in half.
I fainted and was lifted high. I feel
Waist-deep in rain. My face is dry and drawn,
My beauty leaks into the glass like rain.
When first I opened to the sun I thought
My colors would be parched. Where are my bees?
Must I die now? Is this a part of life?

Sometimes I mutter to myself, Where are my bees? That's what I'm missing, just that.

So simple. And this is why I can't think of a
spring holiday. But I'm starting to, despite the
thing sharper than frost, which is always there.

A beautiful Saturday afternoon, and the
sun, at last, is out.

love,

c.

Dear E.,

On the weather channel right now, where
all the announcers are, in their own words,
"passionate about the weather," we are told
that a weather bomb is on its way to Atlantic
Canada and will reach us tonight; but I am
secure and warm in this wonderful old
house—wood fire burning in the downstairs
entrance hall, both cats (Nicholas Nickleby
and his sister, Kate) comfortably stretched on
the rug in front of it, Alasdair writing songs in
his top-floor studio—and I am free for these
moments to be with you.

Certainly I think now, much more than
I used to, about dying as the last living thing
I must do. But without the rather more specific

time frame you have—though even yours and Carol's cannot be specific—my own dying seems altogether theoretical, which it is not.

I wonder if you remember the lines I gave to a character in my novel *Swing Wide the Door,* an actress who drank too much and said to everyone she met, including the gay Salvation Army officer, whose story it is: "What are you dying from? Laughter? Old age? Boredom? Fatigue? Cynicism? Obesity? Stress? Cancer? It's got to be something. We've all got to die of something." And the comment on that: "She's only dying because once upon a time she was born, like the rest of us." That's the way I feel, I guess, but I haven't had to attend any "dress rehearsals" (as you put it) just lately, so it goes on feeling unreal.

Here I am, quoting myself! But then I don't have a wonderful poem to quote, such as Karl Shapiro's, and it's a truly haunting image. Bees. I am lucky. Mine are still around. But not forever. I woke from a reassuring dream two nights ago, and wrote down the sentence I was saying in my sleep (could it have been to you?): "We hope you are happy there, journeying through galaxies with all your friends who are there already. We'll be joining you ourselves one day, which will turn into eternity."

Putting my exact scribbled words (with not a single letter changed) from a sheet of paper into this computer for you now seems like a strange and distant message, but I hope you will receive it differently and with the love that comes with it. May you find peace. You know I'm thinking of you.

Ever . . . ever . . . ever . . .

A.

Dear A.,

How extraordinary that you should dream those words. (Well, no, it isn't. I should have guessed that you, of all people, would have had those thoughts.) Did I ever tell you that, while I do not believe in reincarnation on this earth, I would not be surprised to find that we some-how go on evolving in other galaxies? The image fits in with the strange visions I had

shortly after I started receiving treatment—all
the cosmic patterns and designs—so beautiful
and vividly coloured. When I think of it,
they're a little like the best "trips" described in
Huxley's *The Doors of Perception*.

But while a part of me certainly relates to
the poem Carol quotes, I don't really identify
with the flower Shapiro describes so beautifully.

Right now, I feel that my root system is
doing fine. It's not the season for blooming.
(Or bees.) And I guess I also believe in that
seed far beneath the winter snows, though it
may not fit in very logically with travelling
through galaxies. But for *this* spring, anyway,
who can tell? Even about bees?

Ever . . . ever . . . ever . . .

E.

Even in this new year, which had begun with a
funeral, Elma was able to believe that her own root
system was "doing fine," and Carol could wonder if
a spring holiday might be possible, "despite the thing
sharper than frost" that was ever present.

Because I believed that the language of words

was constantly failing me on this journey with Elma and Carol, a journey that was harder than I knew when I agreed to bear them company, I looked sometimes beyond words to say what I wanted to say, and found it in Alasdair's music. He had written a work entitled *Spirit Room* that I decided to send to Elma, together with his explanatory program note:

> *Spirit Room*, a work for piano and orchestra, was inspired by a dream in which the golden light emanating from beneath a closed door seemed to beckon the dreamer to open it and release the energetic spirit within. This image was the starting-off point for the musical work, which develops its own organic structure free from a sense of programmatic narrative. The first movement is longer and explores a slowly transforming lyrical theme, while the shorter scherzo-like second movement alternates, at a brisk tempo, between a lively tune and subsequent variations of itself.

Elma wrote that she played the work immediately upon receiving it, and, as I learned later, she played it many more times in the three months she had left to live. So obvious was it to her that there was a beckoning light under a door she would one day have to go through, a door that would take her into a brilliant world of colour and energy, that *Spirit Room* became an identifying part of her final quest.

January of that year, however, had been a relatively good month. As Carol had promised, Elma received a galley proof of *Unless*. She had asked to have it sent, fearing she might not live long enough to hold the published novel in her hands.

Dear A.,

I am loving the illicit reading of Carol's novel. Maybe it's the subject matter (a lot to do with mother/daughter relationships); maybe that I'm more focused now that I'm not restricted so much to reading at the end of a working day. But I'd say it's her crowning achievement.

Not to be greedy, but do you have any more short stories kicking around that I could read sometime? My eyesight is quite erratic, so I'm trying to fit in what I can while I can . . .

Ever . . . ever . . . ever . . .

E.

"Short stories kicking around," she had written, and because two, "Her Treasures" and "A Delicate Letter," had appeared in a small New Brunswick literary journal, I sent those first, and then others over the next couple of weeks, stories that had been languishing in a desk drawer for want of finding a home. The two published stories were about women, the third ("Lions at Delos") was about two men, and the fourth ("The Baptism") about a five-year-old boy, baptized ("regenerated and born anew of water" so that he might "die from sin and rise again") by a flushed priest with roving hands.

> Dear A.,
>
> I have only read your stories once so far, which is not enough for a decent evaluation. But I read them immediately after finishing Carol's novel, and felt no sense of drop off— you are marvellous in this medium . . . Please send me more. I'll return them, pay the postage, whatever. They're exactly what I need right now. From a technical point of view also, since they're short, in a good-sized type, lines well-spaced, well laid-out on the page—these

are becoming major considerations if I am to
be able to keep on reading. (And if I can't read,
I might as well not breathe!) The length doesn't
matter nearly so much as the other factors.
Send more! I don't care if they're not what you
think are your best efforts—I'll love them anyway . . . (So far, I'm enjoying you more than
the latest Alice Munro—and I love Alice.)

Elma asked if I was writing anything new, and I
had told her I was doing another draft of *What's
Remembered* (a novel that was published after her
death) and I was working obsessively. The problem
was that I was haunted by the biblical injunction not
to pour new wine into old bottles. The process was
tricky, I related to her, because "I create new characters and then wonder if they will fit into the old
existing form." But Elma assured me that Carol had
once faced and overcome a similar problem when
she had tried to fix and extend something she had
written earlier.

I can imagine it must be hard to do what
Carol called a sort of "darning job." She had

to perform this on one of her novels, which
also needed extra characters, more developed
situations etc. . . . I don't think she ever tried
that again, though it worked out OK—in
fact, I thought it was one of her better ones,
so take heart!

Elma had read only the first of twelve drafts of
What's Remembered, and I had taken her comments
to heart. That fact made me deeply regret that she
did not live long enough to see the work in print. No
reason, of course, for Death to wait or pay attention
to the heavy sound of "deadline," even when that
word comes from a publisher. I thought then of
Emily Dickinson:

Because I could not stop for Death,
He kindly stopped for me;
The carriage held but just ourselves
And Immortality.

THREE

Something has occurred to her—something transparently simple, something she's always known, it seems, but never articulated. Which is that the moment of death occurs while we are still alive. Life marches right up to the wall of that final darkness, one extreme state of being butting against the other. Not even a breath separates them. Not even a blink of the eye. A person can go on and on tuned in to the daily music of food and work and weather and speech right up to the last minute, so that not a single thing gets lost.

—From *The Stone Diaries*

ON THE LAST DAY of January 2002, Elma wrote that her "primary tumour had shrunk to virtually zero, with no activity at all. So no more chemo!" But as January turned into February, the signals grew darker.

Dear A.,

No more chemo is a lovely prospect, indeed, but I must remember that the brain is a whole different story, and it has always been the big problem. No one was really very concerned about the chest tumour, except to radiate it in order to keep it from becoming so large as to be painful. The chemo was to help stop its (lung tumour) metastasizing (say into the other lung), and thus decreasing my general well-being. However, I don't want to sound negative here, and while I could still fly out of the world any time, day or night, without warning, I *hope* one can infer that the radiation worked reasonably well on the brain, since it did on the lung, and has thus bought me a bit of time. Too bad they can't repeat the brain radiation (or won't consider it before a year, anyway) as they could with the chest, but them's the breaks, and I ain't complaining!

Nor am I forgetting that I owe any reprieves as much to the love and support and prayers of my family and friends as I do to luck or good genes—probably way more. So thanks a trillion—and keep those positive thought-waves a-coming. To say nothing of the stories—whee! And I wish you continued high energy and inspiration for the novel, of course.

Ever . . . ever . . . ever . . .

E.

Ever the optimist, despite what she knew was coming, Elma continued to read and to think. Writing to me the next week, she told me she had read two more of my stories "with delight," but "I always need at least two, better three, readings before I fit things together and know my own mind." She had also seen the film version of Annie Proulx's *The Shipping News*, and had admired the characters, who were, she wrote,

> exactly as I had pictured them. And the scenery was beautifully filmed. No wonder in that land of cloud, fog and mirages, that people have "the sight," and the line between so-called truth and fiction almost ceases to exist.
>
> I was also recently blessed by a young Aboriginal woman, someone with "the sight," in an amazingly soothing laying-on-of-hands ceremony, which helps my acceptance a lot . . . There have been revered healers (usually, though not always, female) since pre-recorded history, in every country and culture, though the Christians certainly did their best to stamp them out in Europe and elsewhere.

Her next letter brought disquieting news, which accounted for Carol's not having been directly included in recent exchanges.

Dear A.,

Rather than forwarding e-mails, or sending joint ones, I have been giving Carol brief news and notes about your stories, your and Alasdair's musical activities, the possibility of your novel being published—when will you know, I wonder?—and other anecdotes. This is mostly because she has been in worsening shape, and not up to reading or writing much. Her e-mails to me have mostly been very brief medical reports. Her doctor had actually ordered her to go to Florida for a week between chemo treatments, and she was looking forward to sun and reading. I received the following last night: "We are back, earlier than we'd planned, and I'm not doing terribly well. Starting today, someone is coming to help me with letters and so on. I seem to be sleepy so much of the time."

"Not doing terribly well" means awful. Increasing sleepiness is often a sign that someone has begun to slip away. I feel devastated, but I don't think she is in pain, and going gently into that good night is very often no bad thing.

I, on the other hand, am feeling pretty well, apart from side effects of steroids, which are more of a nuisance than an affliction.

About the scan of my head, done on February 9th, the results should have been available to my doctor today, had she cared to phone . . . I have every intention of phoning *somebody* Thursday or Friday and saying (truthfully) that I really need to know something in terms of how heavy a dose of steroids I should now be on. Could the doctor contact me at least to say "swelling/re-growth not too bad" or "swelling markedly increasing" or whatever. I do not want to wait two weeks to find out this much, even if there is very little they can do about the results, apart from altering the steroid dose.

I must go, but I love you dearly.

Ever . . . ever . . . ever . . .

E.

P.S. I recently came across a poem by Stanley Kunitz, who was interviewed at the Dodge Poetry Festival in 1998, five years after Carol had won her Pulitzer Prize, and almost forty years after he had won his. He was ninety-three at the time of the interview, and still an avid gardener. This particular poem, "The Round," conveys a writer's need for two worlds, and the necessity of pulling down the blinds sometimes on an outer world in order to concentrate on an inner one. Try to find the poem somewhere, if you can; for while it may not be the greatest poem of our time, it resonates on a variety of levels. Kunitz walks about in the early-morning light of his garden, appreciating the flowers he has grown, taking unusual joy in everything around him, but then has to settle again to his work as a writer, where the hard task of shaping words to fit his vision brings him daily challenges and rewards.

Much later, after finding and reading the poem myself, I agreed with Elma on two counts. It may not have been "the greatest poem of our time," but it did convey with a simple and direct beauty "a writer's need for two worlds"—the private retreat, the public persona—how to keep one from intruding on the other, the everlasting challenge.

How often have I sat at my desk, as I do now, like Stanley Kunitz did at ninety-three, thinking myself young because I am only eighty-one, reading aloud my scribbled words, checking the rhythms, looking for sharper images, trying for coherence in a jumble of ideas, writing something down, crossing it out, putting it all into my computer, seeing next the detached formality of a printed page, which makes cruelly evident what still needs work. The other world breaks in—do the laundry, feed the cats, buy groceries for dinner, weed the garden, go to the bank, buy a book, read the newspaper, talk on the telephone, assure friends in letters, either real or virtual, that I am still alive and functioning. The pendulum swings again, and it's back to the messy page, full of corrections, and the new beginning of every day.

Elma's letter was written on Valentine's Day, though she made no reference to the date. While she surely hoped that a new life might also begin for her each day, uncertainty remained.

The lung cancer, which Martin believed came from heavy smoking, had developed independently of the polyps in her colon, and had then spread to her brain, where there were at least seven tumours in different areas. The symptoms had at first included giddiness and a loss of control in her right hand, which led to her being treated with steroids; but as the cancer progressed and the steroids no longer worked, she started to lose her short-term memory, and she would eventually become confused. When she visited her oncologist the following Monday, she had taken a tape recorder. She was trying to understand and be clear about everything.

> Listening to the tape, I get the impression that the doctor hoped some of the brain tumours might have shrunk to nothing (as the lung tumour did) but had not definitely expected that. Mart confirmed my impression. But the neighbour who accompanied me and took notes said *her* impression was that the doctor got just what she was anticipating. So who knows? At least, there was an all-around improvement, and I could hardly ask for more.

At the time of this visit, and because the radiologist had not been able to clarify the results of a scan, Elma had left with the feeling that the information she had was too sketchy to be helpful. The following week, however, she saw her own doctor, and hope was reborn.

> When I asked my doctor yesterday if she
> could do anything, she managed to obtain a
> fax of the scan report within less than an hour.
> It was quite a bit more informative and left me
> feeling more positive and reassured. "No new
> lesions are seen. Considerable improvement
> has occurred, with a substantial reduction in
> volume (i.e., tumour size) though the number
> of lesions has only slightly diminished." At
> least the general tone is favourable.

Fearing she might sound too optimistic about her own health at a time when Carol was in worsening shape, Elma waited for a couple of weeks before writing specifically to Carol, two letters in four days. By this time, however, her own situation had changed yet again, and she felt it important to let Carol know.

Dear Carol,

I have been thinking about you a great deal. I have to say, if I am to go by what my body is telling me right now, I don't think I have much time left, which, at the moment, doesn't seem like much of a tragedy. Of course, when/if I am not in so much pain, I may feel quite differently.

One good thing—since I feel a need to talk to someone in the middle of the night when I start to get scared, and I can't bring myself to deprive Mart (or my various loving and willing friends) of sleep, I have found that I am being forced to talk to God, which seems to work! And at least He/She is not going to lose sleep over it.

The upshot is that I'm still basically very content with my lot. Martin is in for a few rude shocks, though. He always relied on me to remember stuff for him! He's doing OK, and seems a bit less tense. Anyway, I don't want you to feel at all saddened by what's going on (or not) in my brain. I really feel quite happy at present and still very blessed, apart from the physical pain. The mental stuff I can handle, so far. Funny—I thought it would be the other way around.

I have been re-reading *The Stone Diaries*, which I did not appreciate at all properly the first time round. How on earth did you know, at the age you were then, so much about how it feels to be dying?

Saw my oncologist today, and when I asked how fast the symptoms of deterioration (mental and physical) would increase, she said, in effect, "How fast did it happen at the beginning?" To that I replied, "Very fast indeed." Of course, she's not committing herself to anything, but she sort of shrugged and said, "Well, you know that's the way this cancer operates."

When I say physical, I include chest pain from coughing—I have a cold and various other infections—though the pain from what they call TMJ, a disorder of the jaw, is far worse. The chest pain is possibly a consequence of the ribs being broken (well, cracked) through coughing.

I do wish I knew with more precision when and how fast the sky is likely to fall. I want to see my kids again, and they will want to see me, but how to plan for this?

Good night and God bless.

Elma

Dearest Carol (Also Dear A.),

Way back last fall, I wrote you and said I was going to have to decide about whether or not to have my colon removed. In the same letter, I said I was being bothered by something else as well, but I wasn't going into details, since I knew too little, and it was still only in the "something doesn't feel right" stage. I just knew it was either something of no consequence, or far more serious than the colon thing, and it was, of course, my lungs.

Now, once again I sincerely hope I am reading wrongly what my body seems to be telling me. But in case I'm not, let me say again how much it has meant to me (and still does) to have you "hand in hand in our adventure together. Onward!" What I am still praying for is a "good death"—that I will remain accepting and at peace and that above all I will keep my sense of humour.

Carol, you are a candle to light the sun—many suns for many people—and your presence written (in both your letters and your books), physically in the world, and felt (though the latter through a cloud darkly at times) have seen me through the bleakest of times. What would I have done without you? Your friendship has made all the difference between just enduring and enduring with enjoyment, and even joy.

There's a quote somewhere about friendship being a "world without end." I trust ours is. If I say "I won't ever leave you," I sound like Jesus, and even my egotism doesn't stretch that far. But I don't see my leaving you if you ever need me. My concept of space/time precludes that, for one thing. "Eternity in an hour"—or a nanosecond. As far as I'm concerned, it's still and always an adventure together—onward! I'm always there for you—with a candle.

Much love, and gratitude for having had my
life touched by yours,
Elma
P.S. Arthur—of course most of this applies to
you equally. The "adventure together" bit
comes from an inscription Carol wrote to me
in one of her books, the title story of "Dressing
Up," which was my favourite in that collection
for a number of reasons.

Elma sensed that her time would now be very
short; and, sensing something of this myself, I wrote
immediately to Martin. His reply included a direct
message from Elma.

Dear Arthur,
Thank you for your note and your concern.
I knew that it would embrace both of us.
Basically I find that my own moods vary with
Elma's feelings and experiences. Consequently,
most of this year has been quite bearable,
because Elma herself has been so positive in
her attitude . . . When she begins to lose her
grip on what's happening, I find myself silently

pleading, impotently, "Please don't go!" But the saddest times are when I know she's in a lot of physical pain. She surprised herself with the discovery that simple physical pain is more scary, for her, than the loss of mental faculties. So it's more of an agony for the partner as well. And what's causing the serious pain right now? Not the cancer, but the jawbone!

[Addendum by E.: You would think that anyone who has endured pre-antibiotic ear infections, abscessed teeth, and childbirth—the pain of which I thought at the time was unsurvivable—would have a clue. But it wasn't until I realized that given a choice between losing a brain faculty such as, say, my hearing and enduring the pain in my jaw, and realizing that losing hearing would win hands down, that I realized how bad my situation was. Losing my sight would be a tougher call.]

So please join us in a paean of thanks for 21st-century antibiotics and anodynes.

Love,

Martin [and Elma]

It was a further week before Elma felt strong enough to write a letter on her own, this time sending the same one to Carol and me as she sent to a number of other friends, but showing some evidence of an inability to express herself in clear sentences:

All of you, please send some prayers, thought-waves, etc., for my assessment on the 3rd of April. I hadn't realized that I did have some hopes for that very faint light at the end of the tunnel until I've now learned how much faster my brain functions are deteriorating than are my physical, except that they're interdependent, of course—in a sense, everything is a brain function . . . I'm afraid when they assess me now, they'll say—forget it—it's not worth it. (Probably true, too.) But pray that I will accept whatever I'm landed with, and do so with peace and humour.

Love, thanks, and—anyone who wants to even talk to me on the phone, or e-mail me, one last time had better get moving! I'm sorry I'm going to be so disoriented and confused for the rest of the future. Really, so as not to tire myself too much for even talking, I should get you to pick a number or buy a lottery ticket! Getting to see me or talk to me may be a matter of luck!

Right now, I am busy choosing music for my funeral. I think *not* "When the saints go marching in," but I like "So long, it's been good to know ya," or "I've done laid around this ol' town too long, and it seems like it's time to travel on." If you want a tear-jerker, I'm very fond of "Ye Banks and Braes" and also of "Loch Lomond"—"Ye'll tak' the high road . . . and I'll be in Scotland afore ye."

I apologize to those who may feel I'm being a trifle *too* flippant. Sorry, guys, that's my style, it's how I cope, and absolutely no disrespect is meant to anyone or any power.

Pass the word—but discreetly.
Elma

Two days later, I received a note of my own.

Dear A.,

Whatever he may say, Mart is having a very tough time right now—it is finally hitting

him that he *is* going to lose me. I've been trying for ages to get him to believe that this
whole business will be much harder on him
than on me, but men are so *stubborn*—they
have to tough it out. Women have the advantage of being used to talking about their feelings, and accepting emotional support from
groups of friends. Men, in general, it seems to
me, don't have those kinds of friendships;
won't ask for help; won't let themselves break
down. I know there are lots of exceptions, but
I seem to run into the rule—maybe partly
because of my age. Anyway, Mart is going to
need a *lot* of help and feelings of being cared
about in the next year or whatever, and he is
grateful for it, whether he shows it or not. You
are very good about expressing these things.
Also, you have many interests—like music and
the theatre, in fact, literature in general—in
common, so maybe you could drop him an e-
line occasionally? Or a short story? (Only if
you feel like it—I'm not trying to pull a "to
you from failing hands" deal here, as if I were
John McCrae in Flanders Fields!) And do you

have any more stories for *me* while I can still follow a plot line?

Ever . . . ever . . . ever . . .

E.

Dear E.,

I am keeping all fingers and toes crossed that you will hear something reassuring from your assessment tomorrow; and yes, of course, I will keep in touch with Martin, as I will with you through all those ways known to anyone aware that we are more than just physical and material beings. You will be around when I listen to Mahler. You will always be part of my life when I read poetry, especially Hopkins, which I did the other day, reading aloud to myself "The Leaden Echo and the Golden Echo," thinking it was meant for you—"See; not a hair is, not an eyelash, not the least lash lost . . . the thing we freely forfeit is kept with fonder a care, fonder a care kept than we could have kept it." If necessary, I will always remind Martin of these truths, so don't worry.

As for short stories, did I ever send you "Lions at Delos"? You might like that one. I'll print it for you if you haven't got it already.

Any recent news of Carol? I see there is to be a reading in her honour at Harbourfront in Toronto. All sorts of writers will be there, including Michael Ondaatje.

Ever . . . ever . . . ever . . .

A.

Like Elma, Michael had been a student of mine at Bishop's University, but he arrived in 1962, the year after she graduated. Had they been there together, each would have admired the other's gifts, the sensitivity, the intelligence, the rare insights, evidenced at this early age, each of them rejoicing in language. Although she never mentioned it to me in her last years, I like to think that Elma might, at some point, have read these lines from Michael's book of poems *Handwriting*, published in 1998, for she would have greatly admired them, as I do. A teacher can be humbled—this one, anyway—by a former student whose use of English points out "an unknown field or surprising city over the horizon."

It was water in an earlier life I could not take
into my mouth when I was dying. I was
soothed then the way a plant would be,
brushed with a wet cloth, as I reduced all
thought into requests. Take care of this flower.
Less light. Curtain. As I lay there prone during
the long vigil of my friends. The ache of ribs
from too much sleep or fever—bones that pro-
tect the heart and breath in battle, during love
beside another. Saliva, breath, fluids, the soul.
The place bodies meet is the place of escape.

Elma's reply to me showed once more how clear
her critical judgment could be on her good days.
Even as a student, forty years earlier, she had never
been afraid to speak her mind.

Dear A.,
    Yes, I did read "Lions," but though, as I
said at the time, I found the descriptions very
evocative, I also found the story itself a bit
predictable. I preferred "The Baptism,"
which I think you sent at the same time. "Her
Treasures" is still my favourite.

You said all the right things regarding poetry associations and also regarding Mart— he knows a lot of Hopkins by now.

Everybody except me seems to have heard about the release of Carol's book. Can't remember if I told you I got an advance proof from Random House. Have you seen any reviews? I haven't, and would love to know what the word is. I have only read it once, so can't make a final assessment, but so far I think it's her Big One. I loved it. A wonderful note to end on.

Like me, C. goes up and down in wild swings—more down than up. I've told her I'll race her to the bottom of our downhill ski race or whatever this is.

Ever . . . ever . . . ever . . .

E.

I wrote back the next day, unaware that she had asked of me her last question in what was to be her last letter. She was racing Carol to the bottom of the hill and getting there first.

Dear E.,

Yes, you did tell me you had read an advance
proof of Carol's book, and I'm so glad you liked
it; but no, I haven't seen any reviews of it yet.

I stopped writing short stories because I
never seemed to get anywhere with them, but
I'll look to see if I have anything else you
might like to read.

This is your assessment day. I am thinking
of you.

Ever . . . ever . . . ever . . .

A.

It was the day after the April 3rd assessment that
Martin wrote to me and others on Elma's list.

First of all, the radiotherapy specialist stressed
that she continues to feel very encouraged by
the results of the CT scan that was done on
February 9, which showed that all of the brain
tumours have been reduced in size by the
radiotherapy that was performed last fall.

Secondly, she said very firmly that she will
not advise a second round of radiotherapy at

this time, which would involve a high risk of very undesirable side effects, including drastic memory loss and personality change.

This carried an implication that had not occurred to either of us before today: Elma's recent memory loss and disorientation may be in part a side effect of the radiotherapy of last fall, and not simply due to the brain tumours now starting to grow back. In other words, the recent symptoms should not lead us to conclude that the tumours are growing wildly right now. That is good news so far as Elma's current life expectancy is concerned, though, as usual, the doctor would not volunteer any specific estimate. She said very earnestly to Elma, "You have a good quality of life right now." But perhaps this was just because she only saw Elma sitting down: Elma moving around does not look like a well person these days. Or it may be a reflection on the overall health of her other patients.

She has ordered a bone scan, which will take place within a few weeks (to make sure that the recent problems with ribs and jaw are not due to the cancer's having spread to the bones). The last bone scan was done in September, and was negative. There is no reason to think that this one will come back positive. Other than that, she advises us to concentrate on alleviating the jaw pain—with various pain killers for the short run and physiotherapy for the longer run.

There's to be an appointment with the oncologist who is coordinating Elma's cancer treatment on Thursday, April 11. It will represent the next stage in the decision-making.
Martin

[Elma writes: Thanks to all of you for your love and support. I have somewhat mixed feelings at the moment: a definite decision to do something, however risky, always appeals to me. However, the doctor was *very* firm about the danger of more radiotherapy. Basically, she's saying, "You've done marvellously well so far. Why mess with a good thing?"

I want to thank all of you again for being there for me at all times throughout this rather trying—and scary—period, and I know it has been hard on my family and friends as well! We are also grateful for your having left us in peace today—which we needed—though we are anxious to talk to you individually when time and energy permit.

All this sounds so stilted.

Hey guys, I love you all!

Elma]

"I do feel sorry for you reading all this whining," Elma had written in the first of these Staircase Letters, but it was now more than a year later, and neither she nor Carol had ever given a hint of whining. They might have wished for more time to love the world they were in and to finish what they had set out to do, but they never complained. They were making a last journey together, and they would hold fast, as Ulysses did:

> . . . *that which we are, we are;*
> *One equal temper of heroic hearts,*
> *Made weak by time and fate, but strong in will*
> *To strive, to seek, to find, and not to yield.*

A genuine lover of Victorian poetry, the young student Elma and now the older, dying Elma would never dismiss Tennyson as old-fashioned and sentimental, irrelevant in today's sterner world. I am reminded also of Stanley Spencer, the highly regarded British artist, who died almost seventy years after Tennyson. Because he could no longer speak, he wrote down his last words: "Sorrow and sadness is not for me." For Carol and Elma, their message was the same.

Not realizing that what I would be writing next would be my last letter to Elma, I assured her on the same day that she was seeing her oncologist that I was thinking of her.

Dear E.,

I think of you every day, of course, and know that today you are seeing your oncologist, so I will be anxious to hear about that when you or Martin can tell me.

I have started to read *Unless* with real delight. Books have to stand on their own, I know, without the reader having to know much (even anything) about the author; but when a personal thread is there, appreciation can be heightened. Such discipline and freedom in the writing! I am reminded of my friend Joe Plaskett, the artist: when I see his work, I realize more than ever that he, at eighty-three, has the insight and the skills to paint anything he wants to paint, and he does. Carol, too, uses language now in any way she wants, and with an unerring sense for what's right, to say all the perceptive things she has to say, and I am full of admiration.

Today was a real spring day, and I worked in the garden this afternoon. I have aching muscles tonight to prove it! I hope you are having some good days. I'm sure you inspire all those around you.

Ever . . . ever . . . ever . . .

A.

But it was Martin who responded the next day, giving news of Elma to me and a number of her friends.

Hello everyone,

I am writing to let you know that at Elma's appointment with the oncologist, on Thursday afternoon, we turned the corner from active treatment to palliative care.

The bone scan ordered by the radiotherapy specialist will be done next Tuesday, as scheduled. If the result is positive, the doctor has said it will be possible to treat the two very painful sites (rib and jaw) with radiotherapy. But aside from that, the only treatments that will be undertaken will be to relieve pain and discomfort. Elma is being enrolled in the palliative care program of the Winnipeg Health Authority, which is a truly excellent program.

I see now that there would have been an opportunity—late last fall, before the chemo and radiotherapy had completely shrivelled up the primary lung tumour—for metastatic bone cancer to have got started. I think this must be what the doctor suspects. It would certainly explain the severe pain Elma has experienced in those locations. The pain is not nearly so unbearable, now that we have learned how to use Tylenol 3 tablets to best effect. (It means waking her up every four hours to take the pain killers. A bit like getting up to feed a newborn baby.) But we'll move on to morphine next week if that seems to be called for.

The oncologist, who will never speak of expected survival except in terms of averages—quite properly, since that is all that medical science can tell us—was nonetheless very emphatic in saying, "Your family should come and visit you *now*!" Beth and George, as luck would have it, are already flying over from Paris tomorrow.

We came home from the hospital with a walker, which Elma is so far refusing to use, just like her stubborn old dad in his arthritic old age, although she promised she would not emulate him in that respect.

Our love to you all,

Martin

The scheduled appointment with the radiotherapist for the following Tuesday did not take place.

Hello everyone,

I am writing to tell you that our dear Elma died today, Monday, April 15, at 11.45 a.m. Winnipeg time.

The end was very peaceful, and she was free from pain. Standing around the bed with me were our three children, as well as Beth's husband, George, and James's fiancée, Britta. John's wife, Carol, could not be present, but was very much with us in spirit.

After a few minutes of silence, gathered around the bed, we played the CD of Alasdair's *Spirit Room*. It was something that Elma had enjoyed hearing many times, and we could not think of anything more apt than music inspired by a dream of a door opening into the spiritual world.

Her body was taken to the Faculty of Medicine of the University of Manitoba, because she has donated it to be used for research and teaching.

The end came much more swiftly than anyone had anticipated. But on Sunday, when I realized that the end was near, I felt immensely grateful that it was going to be, from then on, really easy for her. Swift or slow was of no consequence.

We are most grateful for all the good thoughts and support we have received from you all over the past months. You have turned what might have been a very bleak time into a time of rich and poignant beauty.

With love and gratitude from us both,
Martin

I agreed with Martin that death's pace at the end was of little consequence. Alasdair's music had ushered Elma into a spirit room of her own, where all her horizons would be blue and bright forever. And listening to *Spirit Room* often since then, I am sure of that.

It was Carol I wrote to immediately, enclosing for her my letter to Martin.

Dear Carol,

Because a number of your letters to Elma over these last several months specifically included me and mine to her included you, and because I can no longer write to her, I give you now what I have just sent to Martin, a finale to our rather extraordinary correspondence, meaning it also for you:

Dear Martin,
I could not account for the sense of total disquiet I felt late yesterday morning and into the afternoon until your letter came this morning, telling me of Elma's death, almost at the exact moment my unease was at its strongest. There is no rational explanation for such mysteries, of course, and I can only tell it to you as a fact; but I am now haunted by what I can only guess at and Elma must now know.

Alasdair was very moved, as I was, to learn that you had all listened to his Spirit Room *just when Elma was entering hers. She had told me several times how much she liked his music and that work, in particular, so it was wonderful that it was there to accompany her . . .*

Though I have not been privileged to meet you, Carol, and your family, except through Elma's eyes, I know how special you all were to her

and must be now for each other, and my heart goes out to all of you in love and sympathy.
Arthur

Dear Arthur,

Thank you so much for sending me your thoughts. It was exactly what I needed, a hand to reach out to and hold on to. I am still unable to believe she is gone; it was so much faster than I imagined, and it was only a week ago that she wrote about the music she wanted to have at the ceremony. I am sure she told all this to Martin, so that her wishes will be known. I wrote him an e-mail yesterday, but am now getting some thoughts down on real paper. How lacking English is in words of consolation! and how unused we are to employing them.

With thanks and warm wishes,
carol

Dear Carol,

I appreciate so much your reply. Your own hand reaching out to me is also special and comforting.

You and Elma were able to share so much on so many levels that I always felt inadequate when I tried to say anything or do anything helpful. But there was/is nothing to say or do: I could only "be," in the hope that would be enough.

Allow me to think of you now, even more, and wish you days of peace.

Sincerely,

Arthur

———

Elma's prediction about how speedily her own cancer would develop compared with Carol's had proven correct; Carol lived courageously for fifteen more months, almost to the day.

From that April 15th of 2002, which marked one death, until July 16th of 2003, which marked the other, I kept in touch with Carol less often but regularly. On one occasion, it was to congratulate her on being nominated for one of the world's great literary prizes, the Booker, to which she responded: "Thank you for such warm words. I am indeed delighted.

And astonished. Three Canadians. Carol." (It may have been accidental, but I like to think she allowed herself a brief moment of pride when she typed her name, for the only time, with a capital *C*.)

On another, it was to say how much I was enjoying *Dressing Up for the Carnival* (stories Elma had also liked very much), particularly "Eros," which was, I told her, a little gem—"so funny, so touching, so sad, so true, and every chosen word exactly where it should be." In it, Ann—a divorced woman who finds herself at a dinner party where the "conversation drifted towards the subject of sexuality"—reflects on her own life, recalling the mysteries of sex in childhood, the comic confusions of adolescence, and the disappointments found in a marriage that failed, despite going with her husband to Paris, the city of lovers, to heal the breach.

In "Love so Fleeting, Love so Fine," another gem in the book, a man's vulnerable heart is exposed just because he spots a hand-printed, fairly crude sign in the window of an orthopedic shoe store in downtown Winnipeg that reads WENDY IS BACK. Who but Carol could make us see how something so apparently insignificant—who is Wendy, anyway, and why should we care?—could "cut deeply into his heart and widen for an instant the eye of the comprehended world"?

Yet this is what Carol does, over and over again, in her stories. The world in a grain of sand. Blake would have understood.

There was also her play *Thirteen Hands*, which I read with admiration and joy:

> You got it all absolutely right, line after line
> after line, character after character, scene after
> scene, absolutely bang-on all the time. I wish
> I were still directing plays in universities,
> which is what I used to do, as Elma must have
> told you, for I would want to direct yours;
> but how happy I am at my age still to be dis-
> covering such wonders as your play.

Further nominations for the Giller and the Governor General's and the Commonwealth Writers' Prize did not get turned into awards, but when the Giller jury overlooked *Unless* in favour of *The Polished Hoe* by Austin Clarke, I learned much later from one of Carol's friends how she handled rejection and made clear her sense of human values. Having made the journey to Toronto with her daughter Meg and Meg's new baby, she was able to retire to their room at the Four Seasons Hotel, not long after hearing the outcome. Once there, she embraced her new grandchild and put disappointment behind her. The baby she held in her arms provided a joy deeper than any prize the world could possibly bestow.

Whenever I would send an e-mail, I would tell Carol to save her energies and not write back, but she ignored all such suggestions, of course, as she did again that Christmas:

> Dear Carol,
>
> You probably get 3,683 Christmas cards and e-mails from all your friends and admirers the world over, but may I just make that number 3,684 when I tell you I am thinking of you and sending only warm wishes for your well-being. I hope you will continue to feel supported by the love of those who surround you.
>
> As ever,
>
> Arthur

Arthur,

I was just thinking of you this morning,
and so it was wonderful to receive your greet-
ings. I wish you a joyous holiday. Christmas
always seems to me terribly hectic, but then it
just settles down into quietness and spontane-
ity, and that is where we are at the moment.
Blessings in the new year.
carol

In the new year I was prompted to write again
about something I knew she would understand.

Dear Carol,

Since I can't tell Elma, may I tell you—
and you will appreciate it, even be amused by
it, because I am now seventy-seven and a bit
old to be starting all this stuff—that I have
been dealing for these last many months with
the very good editor and publisher of
Cormorant Books in Toronto, Marc Côté,
and it seems that the novel *What's
Remembered* I have been working on for several years will get published. Elma had read a

previous draft and had helped me with it enormously.

Please don't spend your energies writing back. My computer will be able to tell if this gets through to you, and that's all I need to know. I do hope you are feeling reasonably well these days. You inspire so many everywhere by being you.

As ever,
Arthur

I could never have guessed that the letter she wrote back the next day would be her last to me. Pure Carol. Pure gold.

Dear Arthur,

Thank you for your warm words. I must admit that I hooted and hopped about in delight and surprise!

Congratulations on being seventy-seven, such a silvery age, and on having a nearly completed manuscript (though I can't imagine why such an accomplished person would want to write a novel). I love the state of being

nearly at the end, when I have the sense of
darning a sock. It's almost like flying. I
believe that metaphor needs some work.
Anyway, good luck with it.

    All best,

carol

Hooting . . . hopping . . . darning a sock . . . flying. Those words say it all—the natural laughter, the
springing joy, the connection to life's simplicities, the
soaring into a bigger world of love. That was Carol
in her life and in her work, so that when she died that
summer, on July 16th, 2003, at the age of sixty-eight,
all those who knew her or had read her books felt the
loss personally.

    I wrote immediately to Carol's family, even
when I knew words would be of little use.

Dear all of you in Carol's family,

    Like thousands of others everywhere, I feel
devastated by the news of Carol's death. She
and Elma and I were linked in a deeply personal way over many months, and when Elma
died in April of last year, it was Carol I thought

of and wrote to immediately. Her generous reply was to tell me that was exactly what she needed—"a hand to reach out to and hold on to."

I feel grateful to have shared what I shared with Carol, but what she gave me was always far more.

Please accept my heartfelt sympathy.

Sincerely,

Arthur

"Where are my bees? Must I die now? Is this a part of life?" Carol had asked, and she had been answered.

Elma had also asked and been answered.

My turn will come next.

For Emily Dickinson, these are mysteries:

The murmur of a bee
A witchcraft yieldeth me.
If any ask me why,
'T were easier to die
Than tell.

I think now about my own dying much more than I used to. I hope, when it comes, that all those I love will move past darkness into their own light, convinced that I may already have moved into mine, as I feel sure Elma and Carol have moved into theirs. In this, they have been my teachers, forever pointing out "a surprising city over the horizon."

To this point I had borne Carol and Elma company as best I could on their hard and dangerous journey, but forever falling short of their courage. Truly, they had given their straight account without delay and were now in their spirit room, a place of light and energy, free of pain, a place of love.

What now will I say at my end—that I need more time for love, or that I used the time I was given?

Still is my heart. It is awaiting its hour!
Everywhere the lovely earth blossoms forth in
    spring
And grows green anew! Everywhere, for ever,
Horizons are blue and bright! For ever and ever.

    Ewig . . . ewig . . . ewig . . .

ARTHUR MOTYER was born in Bermuda and now lives in Sackville, New Brunswick. Rhodes scholar, Member of the Order of New Brunswick and Professor Emeritus of English at Mount Allison University, he also wrote the novel *What's Remembered*.

ELMA GERWIN was active for two decades in literacy initiatives, and she was recognized as one of Canada's top five educators with a Canada Post Literacy Award. A long-time Winnipeg resident, she was married and had three children. She died in 2002.

CAROL SHIELDS was the beloved and award-winning author of more than twenty books. She died in 2003, leaving behind a husband, five children and twelve grandchildren.